Music in Ancient Greece

Classical World Series

Music in Ancient Greece

Melody, Rhythm and Life

Spencer A. Klavan

BLOOMSBURY ACADEMIC

LONDON • NEW YORK • OXFORD • NEW DELHI • SYDNEY

BLOOMSBURY ACADEMIC
Bloomsbury Publishing Plc
50 Bedford Square, London, WC1B 3DP, UK
1385 Broadway, New York, NY 10018, USA

BLOOMSBURY, BLOOMSBURY ACADEMIC and the Diana logo are trademarks of
Bloomsbury Publishing Plc

First published in Great Britain 2021

Cover design: Terry Woodley
Cover image © World History Archive/Alamy Stock Photo

A catalogue record for this book is available from the British Library.

Library of Congress Cataloging-in-Publication Data
Names: Klavan, Spencer A. (Spencer Andrew), 1990– author.
Title: Music in ancient Greece : melody, rhythm and life / Spencer A. Klavan.
Description: New York : Bloomsbury Academic, 2021. | Series: Classical world | Includes bibliographical
references and index. | Summary: "Life in ancient Greece was musical life. Soloists competed onstage for
popular accolades, becoming centrepieces for cultural conversation and even leading Plato to recommend
that certain forms of music be banned from his ideal society. And the music didn't stop when the audience
left the theatre: melody and rhythm were woven into the whole fabric of daily existence for the Greeks.
Vocal and instrumental songs were part of religious rituals, dramatic performances, dinner parties, and even
military campaigns. Like Detroit in the 1960s or Vienna in the 18th century, Athens in the 400s BC was the
hotspot where celebrated artists collaborated and diverse strands of musical tradition converged. The
conversations and innovations that unfolded there would lay the groundwork for musical theory and practice
in Greece and Rome for centuries to come. In this perfectly pitched introduction, Spencer Klavan explores
Greek music's origins, forms, and place in society. In recent years, state-of-the-art research and digital
technology have enabled us to decipher and understand Greek music with unprecedented precision. Yet
many readers today cannot access the resources that would enable them to grapple with this richly
rewarding subject. Arcane technical details and obscure jargon veil the subject – it is rarely known, for
instance, that authentic melodies still survive from antiquity, helping us to imagine the vivid soundscapes of
the Classical and Hellenistic eras. Music in Ancient Greece and Beyond distils the latest discoveries into
vivid prose so readers can come to grips with the basics as never before. With the tools in this book,
beginners and specialists alike will learn to hear the ancient world afresh and come away with a new,
musical perspective on their favourite classical texts"– Provided by publisher.
Identifiers: LCCN 2020040456 (print) | LCCN 2020040457 (ebook) | ISBN 9781350119949 (hardcover) |
ISBN 9781350119925 (paperback) | ISBN 9781350119956 (epub) | ISBN 9781350119970 (ebook)
Subjects: LCSH: Music, Greek and Roman–History and criticism. | Musical instruments, Ancient–Greece.
Classification: LCC ML169 .K53 2021 (print) | LCC ML169 (ebook) | DDC 780.938—dc23
LC record available at https://lccn.loc.gov/2020040456
LC ebook record available at https://lccn.loc.gov/2020040457

ISBN: HB: 978-1-3501-1994-9
       PB: 978-1-3501-1992-5
       ePDF: 978-1-3501-1997-0
       eBook: 978-1-3501-1995-6

Series: Classical World

Typeset by RefineCatch Limited, Bungay, Suffolk

To find out more about our authors and books visit www.bloomsbury.com
and sign up for our newsletters.

For Barnaby Taylor and Armand D'Angour:
You believed I could learn, and that is why I did.

Contents

Figures

Timeline

c. 1400 BC   Date of the world's earliest known musical notation, from the ancient city of Ugarit in what is now Syria.

670s BC   Rough date of the first *kithara* competitions at Sparta's Carneia festival, of which the famous Terpander is said to have been the first winner.

566 BC   Athenian tyrant Peisistratus re-organizes and revitalizes the Panathenaic Games, a festival in honour of Athena held every four years, including prominent musical competitions.

534 (or 531) BC   Peisistratus re-institutes the City Dionysia festival, where tragedies are performed in competition for the top prize.

510–508 BC   Deposition of Peisistratid tyranny.

499–493 BC   A conflict known as the Ionian Revolt draws Greek city-states into conflict with Persia and Asia Minor.

486 BC   Comedy competitions are introduced to the City Dionysia.

c. 480 BC   Creation and use of 'Paestum pipes,' some of our oldest surviving archaeological examples of ancient Greek instruments.

480–479 BC   Persian monarch Xerxes leads an expedition against independent Greek city-states and is rebuffed, ushering in an age of Athenian cultural flourishing and beginning what is traditionally labelled the Classical Period.

472 BC   Début performance of Aeschylus' *Persians*, the first surviving Greek tragedy, at the City Dionysia festival. The theme is Athens' victory over Persia as seen through the eyes of the defeated Persian king, Xerxes, and his retinue.

442 BC   Comedy is introduced to the Lenaea Festival at Athens.

408 BC   Début performance of Euripides' *Orestes*, the only surviving fifh-century tragedy for which some original music is (possibly) preserved.

405 BC   Début performance of Euripides' *Bacchae*, the last surviving Greek tragedy. The theme is a hostile takeover of Thebes by the god of frenzy and theatre, Dionysus.

c. **200** BC   Music which seems to be from Euripides' *Orestes* is written down by an unknown scribe on a papyrus partially preserved as Pap. Vienna 2315.

First or second century AD   Creation of the Seikilos Epitaph, a tomb engraving in what is now Turkey containing some of our clearest ancient rhythmic and melodic notation.

Introduction: Origins and Beginnings

What this book is about

Music has always been with us. Even in prehistoric caves in Spain (the Caves of El Cogul) and Italy (the Grotta dell'Addaura), we can see depictions of dancing people painted onto the walls. And to this day there is no known culture in the world that lacks a tradition of singing, chanting, playing instruments, or moving to a beat. The earliest known form of written musical notation is carved into a clay tablet from around 1400 BC in the ancient city of Ugarit (now Syria). But that's many thousands of years later than the aforementioned cave paintings, a fact from which we learn something important: music itself is much older than music notation. The vast majority of ancient music left behind no trace for historians to study. There are still songs being sung today that will never get written down – think of the rhymes you used to chant as a kid on the playground, or the private melodies that some parents make up and sing to their babies. These unwritten tunes might be passed down within families, or after a short while they might vanish forever. But whether written or not, music is a fundamental component of human life. Wherever there are people, they sing and dance together.

This book is first and foremost about ancient Athens – the voting citizens, the rich matrons, the enterprising prostitutes, the slaves, the immigrants, the children, and everyone else who lived together in a form of legally and culturally organized life called a city-state (or in Greek, a *polis*). Athens is near the eastern tip of Greece, the first major city one would encounter if travelling into Europe from Turkey or elsewhere in the Middle East. In the ancient world it was often a hub for commerce, travel, and trade among the many cultures that would move between those eastern regions and the communities of what is now Europe. This became especially true during the fifth century BC, in between 479 (when a coalition of Greek city-states managed to fend off colonization by the massive Persian Empire) and 404 (when Athens was forced under siege to surrender to Sparta, its major rival for power in Greece, at the end of the conflict between them called the Peloponnesian War).

The period before the Greek victory over Persia in 479 is usually called the 'Archaic' period, whereas the period after is called the 'Classical' period. Here we come up against a problem: as will soon become clear, the Classical period was a time of tremendous cultural flourishing, during which many of the developments that interest us took place. But it was also, crucially, *not* the period during which many of our sources about music were written. Quite a few great poets (such as composers of tragedy like Aeschylus, Sophocles, and Euripides, or of lyric like Pindar and Bacchylides) and historians (Herodotus and Thucydides chief among them) did leave written records of their work that survive to this day. But plenty of others, including many musicians and musical philosophers (Damon of Athens, Timotheus of Miletus, Lasus of Hermione, and the rest whom we will meet in this book) left nothing or only a few fragments.

We can ameliorate the situation somewhat by reading reports from philosophers such as Plato, who was born in the 420s BC and wrote reflections on fifth-century Athenian life throughout his career, though that career itself extended well into the fourth century. Other fourth-century writers, such as the philosopher and music theorist Aristoxenus, paid minute and careful attention to musical forms which probably originated, at least in part, during the fifth century and earlier. But in each of these cases we have to be careful: the echoes of history get fainter as each year passes, and methods of reporting were much less reliable in the ancient world than they are today. Besides which, every author has an agenda: Plato's opus was devoted, broadly speaking, more to philosophical than to musical accuracy. And Aristoxenus was attempting to craft a standard system for organizing musical practices that were, in real life, much more unruly and varied than he often let on. Similar warnings apply to Plato's student Aristotle, who wrote even later than his teacher, and to theorists like Dionysius of Halicarnassus – who was later still, and whose expertize in technical matters was somewhat limited.[1] So although we are not at a loss for sources, we will always have to think in this book about who's telling us the story, and be cautious about whose reports we take at face value. But through the late reports, the fractured testimonies, and the eyewitness accounts, we can get something like a glimpse at what happened to music in Athens during the fifth century and in the Greek-speaking world afterwards.

During the Classical period itself, Athens was buzzing with artistic and intellectual activity. Every so often in history, stars align and one city becomes a nexus where people from around the world meet, collaborate, and share new ideas – think of Detroit in the Motown explosion of the 1960s or Vienna in the eighteenth-century heyday of Classical music. That's what Athens was like in the 400s: electric with new forms of politics, debate, and art. Flushed with the exhilaration of facing down a Persian onslaught, the Athenians came to see themselves as world leaders and to pride themselves on being at the cutting edge of culture. 'Everything comes from every city into ours,' said the Athenian general and statesman Pericles in 431 BC. 'We reap the fruits of other cultures just as naturally as we reap our own.'[2]

Pericles was overstating the case quite a bit, but it's true that Athens learned a great deal from the societies surrounding it (more than Pericles himself might have liked to admit). In the 400s, Athenian culture became a kind of crucible in which all sorts of musical traditions merged to form something radically new and exciting. The advancements made in musical theory and practice during that time caught on all around the Mediterranean. In some cases they radiated even further outwards to influence other cultures and subsequent generations – the Romans, especially, adopted many Greek musical practices and spread them throughout the ancient world.

That is why ultimately, though this book tends to focus on Athens, it's about more than just Athenian music. As we'll see throughout these pages, Greece was the starting point for a host of hugely important developments in music history, many of which endure to this day and have had major effects even on the music that remains popular in the modern West. From Shostakovich to Skrillex, from Bach to Beyoncé and in between, almost no part of Western music history is untouched by the musical legacy of ancient Greece.

This is not to say that Athens was the be-all and end-all of ancient music. Just the opposite: precisely because it was so abuzz with cultural commerce, Athens was indebted to a huge range of practices and ideas which weren't at all Athenian or even Greek in origin. There is a wealth of valuable and significant music history to learn from before and beyond Athens, and plenty more that we simply will never know. Again, think how often music disappears without ever being written down or written about – if that's still true today, it's even more true for the many highly refined musical cultures which existed before Greece and which, for one reason or another, haven't left the same kind of historical record that Greece did. We're lucky that we have so much from ancient Athens, but even so we need to qualify what we do have with an awareness of all that came before and all that has been lost. We begin, then, by surveying some of what we know – and what we wish we knew – about the music that came into Athens from older traditions around the world.

Influences

One region whose music was certainly influential in antiquity was the vast expanse of realms and kingdoms known today as the 'Near East.' This wasn't just one big block of land: it was a complicated patchwork of sprawling empires that jockeyed for power across Mesopotamia from as early as the 3000s BC. There were the Babylonians and the Assyrians, whose monarchs left behind imposing monuments, some of them still standing now, over all the huge territories that they conquered. There were the Israelites, a small but defiant race of monotheists who staked their claim to a territory beside the Dead Sea – their descendants, the

Jewish people, are of course still thriving and practising their religion around the world. Then there were the Lydians, who ruled in Asia Minor (now Turkey) from about 1200 until 547 BC, when they would be conquered by the Persians. The wealth and sophistication of Persian culture, for its part, is on display even now in the immense remains of the Persian royal complex known as Persepolis, which people still visit in modern-day Iran. It was the Persians that lost the wars against Athens between 490 and 479, the opening of the Classical period. But even before the Persian wars, contact with the civilizations of the East played a major role in setting the scene for the fifth-century cultural explosion.

It stands to reason that encounters with Persia and the Near East would have galvanized Greek musical culture, because all of the societies mentioned above were alive with song and dance. The lyrics to many of ancient Israel's greatest hymns were written down and survive in the book of the Bible called 'Psalms' – the Hebrew title of this book, *Tehillim*, simply means 'worship songs'. Tradition holds that many of these songs were written by the greatest king of Israel, David, who reigned during the tenth century BC and was known for the ecstatic dancing and singing with which he worshipped God (see the Bible's Second Book of Samuel, Chapter Six). Later, King Sargon II of Assyria (who reigned between 722 and 705 BC) left behind an inscription claiming that he gathered 'princes of the four regions of the globe' for 'a feast of music' in his palace.[3] Monarchs like Sargon prided themselves in assembling performers and musicians from the many cities within their power, as a display of how widely their empires ranged and how completely their own capital cities excelled the rest. Artists of all kinds, then, gathered from around the world in the great courts of ancient Mesopotamia and the Levant (the region on the east coast of the Mediterranean where Israel, Syria, Lebanon, and Jordan are found today). These massive royal complexes were centres of diverse and innovative musical culture.

From very early on, Eastern communities were doing business and sharing ideas with Greece. The Levant is only a short journey away from Athens by sea, and Asia Minor with its rich Lydian culture was separated from Europe by nothing more than a tiny strip of water called the

Hellespont. Especially in the eighth and seventh centuries, Greek musicians seem to have taken cues from their neighbours in the East. There are some snatches of Archaic poetry which may indicate that Lydian harps were popular in that period among the Greek male gentry – although on vase paintings from the Classical period, harps are represented as an instrument for women. In any case, Archaic Greeks certainly did have their own stringed instrument, lower-toned than the Lydian harp: the long seven-stringed *barbitos*. The Greek court songwriter Pindar thought that Terpander (one of the first and best-known Greek musicians) created the *barbitos* after 'hearing the lofty harp strummed at Lydian drinking parties.'[4] Whether or not it really was Terpander who invented the *barbitos*, it's clear that Greek musical culture before the fifth century grew and flourished in dynamic exchange with the thriving cultures of Lydia and Assyria.

One important place where Greek musicians met their fellow artists from the East was the island of Lesbos. That's where Terpander himself was from, along with many of the other greats of the Archaic period. The people on Lesbos spoke Greek, but the island was right off the coast of Asia Minor, putting it closer to Lydia than to mainland Greece and making it a perfect meeting place for singers from all around the Mediterranean. The celebrities from that time in Lesbos are among the most famous of all Greek history: Sappho, especially, made such a name for herself that her admirers used to say she was one of the elegant goddesses of song and poetry known as Muses.[5] Sappho wrote some of the most enduring love songs of her day – or any day, for that matter. The fragments of her work that still survive have been translated into English by famous poets – like the nineteenth-century English writer Christina Rosetti, for example. Or the twentieth- and twenty-first-century Classicist Anita George, who begins one translation of Sappho with the evocative line, 'you: an Achilles' apple / Blushing sweet on a high branch / At the tip of the tallest tree.'[6]

Students today usually read these words in print, as if they were poems meant to be written down in books. But in fact they're song lyrics, and the tradition of poetry that they belong to is called 'lyric' poetry because originally it would have been sung along with a class of stringed instrument called the 'lyre' (more on this in Chapter 2). Sappho's sensuous odes would have been sung at drinking parties (Greek *symposia* – see Chapter 3), and other compositions of hers would likely have been learned by choruses of young girls and performed at public festivals (see Chapter 4). The same is true of Sappho's fellow Lesbian musicians such as Terpander and, a little later, the younger singer Alcaeus. The tight community of artists on Lesbos shared ideas and techniques amongst themselves, but they also learned from their eastern neighbours, making for a two-way international exchange of instruments and songs.

There was cultural crossover going on within Greece, too. Terpander, for one, was famous for having travelled west from Lesbos to the Greek city-state of Sparta. There he was said to have inaugurated the musical competitions held at a festival for Apollo (god of music and medicine) called the Carneia. As often happens in the early history of Greece, it's hard to tell here where fiction ends and fact begins. There definitely was a contest at the Carneia in which performers would sing to their own accompaniment on the lyre and compete for prizes. Terpander is named as the winner in a list from the first of these contests in the 670s BC.[7] He certainly composed for, and played on, the *kithara* – an elaborate professional-grade lyre for concert performance. There are stories (again, quite possibly fictional) that Terpander actually invented the *kithara* too, and it's even possible (although far from certain) that he also wrote and played music for the *auloi* (singular *aulos*), a set of double-pipes which, along with the lyre, was the other major concert instrument of Greek tradition. Whether or not Terpander played the *auloi*, the pipes rivalled (or in some instances even surpassed) the *kithara* as the instrument of competition performance, festival song, and high art in Greece.

But whether or not Terpander was really the founder of the Carneia competition depends on how seriously we take the stories that his admirers told about him. Greek audiences loved their music, and they told all sorts of stories about their favourite singers. As mentioned already, Sappho was counted among the Muses. And the most famous Greek bard of all, Homer, was sometimes said to have been the son of gods. So lots of Terpander's biography is probably just hype and publicity, not unlike the urban legends we tell today – the American blues singer Bob Johnson, for example, was fabled to have sold his soul to the devil in exchange for unmatchable guitar skills. Even if no one really believes that story, it tells us something about Johnson's reputation as a performer. In the same way, even if Terpander didn't actually found the Carneian contest, the story gives us a sense of what a trailblazer he was. But we know that he certainly did compete at the Carneia, thus helping bring the sounds of Lesbos to the militaristic culture of Sparta.

Sparta took its music very seriously. Here again it's hard to tell the truth from the tall tales, because the ancient Spartans didn't write very much down. That means most of what we know about them is based on reports from outsiders like the Athenians, who saw Sparta as a fierce kingdom of uncompromising warriors. The cartoonishly blood-soaked movie *300* exemplifies the exaggerated image of the Spartans that still survives to this day: helmet-clad he-men in bristling regiments, with hearts and sinews as hard as their spearpoints. This is surely a caricature. But it does seem that Spartan life was harshly regulated, ruled by a strict sense of discipline on the concert stage as well as on the battlefield. Society in Sparta was broken up into immutable social classes, and this hierarchy was so rigidly enforced that those in the lowest ranks (the serf class race known as 'Helots') were forbidden from singing the most celebrated songs.[8] Only free men could sing music by the likes of Alcman and Terpander, or by the native Spartan composer Tyrtaeus. Tyrtaeus wrote rousing military anthems to be sung on the battlefield, and a fair amount of the music written in Sparta was probably meant to be played on pipes as the army marched to war. The historian Thucydides writes that the regular beat of pipe music kept the Spartan army stepping in time, and the later (second-century-AD) writer Aulus Gellius tells us that the melody of pipes steadied soldiers' hearts so they could face down enemies with cold determination.[9]

What's next

Music was everywhere in ancient Greek life, and this introduction barely scratches the surface. What follows is a musical tour of Greece with special focus on Athens and its surrounding environs: the religious ceremonies, choral rites of passage, theatrical events, drinking parties, and countless other occasions at which pipe music, strings, dance, and singing could be heard and seen. Chapter 2 is about the history and cultural significance of instruments like the *kithara* and *auloi*. Music competitions like the Carneia will come back up in Chapter 3, which discusses the many occasions for which Greek music was composed and the venues in which it was performed. And Chapters 4, 5, and 6 will be about three of the most influential strands of Greek thought about music – how it relates to education, politics, and the heavens. Chapters 7 and 8 are for the reader interested in how melody and rhythm actually worked in Greece: they discuss the surviving theory and notation which let us reconstruct snatches of real song from Greek antiquity. The final chapter, Chapter 9, will indicate some ways in which the ideas and practices covered in the rest of the book made a lasting impact on cultures that came after Greece, including the many cultures of today's world.

But first, Athens. How did artists and traditions from all around the Mediterranean find their way to one rocky little town in the east of Greece? There are more answers to that question than can possibly be summarized here, and still more that we will probably never know. But one crucial place where musicians could cross paths was at festivals. In Archaic Greece, festivals meant entertainment, and entertainment meant competition. There were gala contests all over the Greek mainland – I've already mentioned an important Spartan one, the Carneia, and there were four other major ones outside of Athens. There were the Pythian Games at Delphi, a city of sheer cliff-faces where prophets served the god Apollo and proclaimed his oracular predictions. On the Peloponnesus (the same southern peninsula where Sparta was) there were the Isthmian Games and the Nemean Games, respectively held near the cities of Corinth and Nemea. And of course there were the Olympic Games – then held every four years at Olympia in the Western Peloponnesus, and now resurrected in modern form at major cities across the whole world.

Like today's Olympics, all of these festivals featured athletes who came from far and wide to face one another down – there were races by chariot and on foot, throwing contests with spears (javelins) and stone discs (discuses), and all sorts of other feats. And though winners did get physical prizes – expensive earthenware trophies, for example, or luxurious olive oil, or the famous crown of laurel leaves – they were also very often celebrated with victory songs called 'epinicians' (a Greek word meaning roughly 'on the occasion of victory'). These were elaborate poems composed in intricate rhythmic patterns, sung by choruses (or in some cases solo), set to melodies on stringed instruments, and commissioned by wealthy winners to praise their achievements. Some of Greece's greatest artists – Pindar and Bacchylides in the late Archaic and early Classical period, for example, and before them Ibycus and Simonides – wrote epinicians, and probably performed them too. But musicians didn't only celebrate other people's successes – they also competed in tournaments of their own. Many of these festivals offered prizes for the best composition and performance on *kithara* and *auloi*. The winners' names were carved into stone, meaning we can still read some of them to this day.

Enter Peisistratus, an autocrat who seized control of Athens during much of the time between the years 560 and 527 BC. In Greek terms, Peisistratus was called a 'tyrant' – that is, he used force to take absolute power over Athens. He wanted to make a name for himself and his city-state on the world stage, and one of the ways he decided to go about it was by bringing Athens' festival culture up to snuff. Much like the Olympics today, Greek festivals were a chance for the host city to boost its visibility, foster diplomatic relations, and show off its local culture. Besides which, monarchs who ruled by coup, as Peisistratus did, always needed ways to shore up support and popularity against other factions who stood poised to steal back leadership of the state. One excellent way to win favour with your subjects is to throw them a giant party that shows how rich and strong you are. So Peisistratus poured funds and effort into revitalizing both the City Dionysus, the annual theatrical festival which honoured the god Dionysus, and the Panathenaia, a festival in honour of Athens' patron goddess, Athena. The Greater Panathenaia ran every four years, and during the intervening three years came a toned-down version called the Lesser Panathenaia – together, they were tailor-made to put Athens on a par with the cities around it. The Panathenaia had sports, music, religious worship – everything essential for spectacular civic self-promotion. The closest modern analogue would be a cross between St. Patrick's Day, the Super Bowl, and a church service on Easter Sunday. It was a massive gathering that brought Greeks together and helped the people of Athens to build solidarity and cultural identity with one another. Shared music is one of the best ways to build common ground: hence the performance of national anthems at sporting events, or school songs sung at the beginning of assemblies. Peisistratus knew that a regular tradition of musical performance would go a long way towards making Athens a force to be reckoned with.

One of the biggest successes in that department was the recitation of poetry composed by the aforementioned Homer. Homer is perhaps the most celebrated, and almost certainly the oldest, artist whose work survives from ancient Greece. And because he's so old, scholars aren't sure whether he was even a real person. What we know is that, long before the Archaic period, singers were travelling around Greece singing a particular kind of music that would come to be known as *epos* (from which we get our modern word 'epic'). *Epos* had its own kind of rhythm (called 'dactylic hexameter' – more on that in Chapter 8), and the songs these singers performed were fantastic tales of heroes, quests, gods, and monsters – the great myths and adventures for which Greece is still known. The songs were engrossing, hypnotic, and nail-bitingly entertaining; they kept audiences riveted for hours on end. Their tunes were probably pretty simple, and may have come with instrumentation on a *barbitos* or similar stringed instrument. At some point during the late eighth century (probably – it might have been the ninth or the seventh), there emerged from among these many songs two very long, continuous epics: the *Iliad* and the *Odyssey*. The first was a battle legend about Achilles, the Greek hero so powerful that entire armies depended on his strength, and the war in which he fought against the city of Troy in Asia Minor. The second was an adventure story about another Greek solider, Odysseus, and his long journey home after that same war. Scholars have argued for centuries about whether these poems were composed by one man or stitched together by many men in several stages. But they do seem to have been preserved through the eighth and seventh centuries on an eastern Greek island called Chios, handed down from generation to generation among a guild of singers called the Homeridae.

So by the time Peisistratus came along, something like what we now call the *Iliad* and the *Odyssey* was being sung (without a written text) by some very skilful bards who considered themselves heirs of a great poet called Homer. It seems like Peisistratus might have seen potential in these small-town stars, and he had the Homeric poems performed at the Panathenaia. This kind of thing still happens: local musical artists can always be picked up by wealthy patrons and get their work distributed to a wider audience, as when a local indie artist gets picked up by a big label and quickly turns into a household name, or when YouTube sensations build up their own private fanbase before scoring more prestigious distribution worldwide. At the Panathenaia, the Homeric poems became the enormous hits that they would be forever afterwards. The competitions probably also helped standardize the songs for mass distribution: if everyone simply sings from memory, then different people are likely to sing slightly different versions. But at festivals like the Panathenaia, performers needed an official version that everyone could agree on, which is why Athens might have been the first place where the entire *Iliad* and *Odyssey* were written down.[10] At some point the lyre was left behind and performers simply chanted the words aloud in a kind of sing-song voice. But the performance of Homer remained one of Athens' most celebrated musical claims to fame, and the Panathenaia put Athens on Greece's cultural map in a serious way.

There were also, of course, epinicians and contests in *kithara-* and *aulos*-playing, as in the other festivals all over Greece. Pindar and Bacchylides both wrote songs to be sung at Athens, and compositions by Terpander and Alcman made their way there too. Under Peisistratus and his son Hipparchus, the city gained a new sense of unity and civic pride. Even after the Peisistratids were deposed for good (between 510 and 508 BC), Athens remained a formidable centre of cultural commerce in its own right, so that musicians started flocking there to make a name for themselves.

One such musician was Lasus of Hermione (from the Argolid, a region of the Peloponnesus), who came to Athens by invitation of Hipparchus and made a name for himself composing a kind of song called a 'dithyramb.' These were choral odes, sung by groups of dancing men and usually meant to celebrate the god Dionysus. Lasus remained in Athens after 508 and became a major figure on the Greek concert stage, establishing new competitions just for dithyrambs and writing what may well have been Greece's first ever book on music – he was probably also one of Pindar's teachers.[11] Lasus was part of a growing community of multitalented artists within Athens who not only wrote music of their own, but also passed on their knowledge to pupils and theorized about best practices for composition and performance.

When Greece won its wars against Persia in 479 and Athens started to think of itself as the central hub of the cultural world, this local community of artists and thinkers was already starting to take off. All it took was winning the war for things really to explode: thrilled with its own success and newly re-established as a democracy, Athens came to see itself as the world centre for commerce and art that Pericles would eventually boast about in 431.

Of course, even while all this local buzz was developing, ideas kept flowing into Athens from outside as well. One crucial but mysterious figure who made a huge impact all over Greece (and beyond it too) was Pythagoras, from the Greek island of Samos in the far east of the Aegean (just off the coast of Asia Minor). Anyone who has ever tried to find the hypotenuse of a right triangle knows Pythagoras from the theorem that bears his name – he's perhaps best known as a mathematician and the bane of teenage geometers. But in fact, since he never wrote anything down, no one quite knows what Pythagoras really did discover, and what was only attributed to him by his many followers. He was a philosopher who lived between about 570 and 495 BC, when a few very sophisticated schools of philosophy were growing up in the Eastern Aegean (called Ionia) and in Greek-speaking colonies throughout Southern Italy (especially in a town called Elea). To his devotees, Pythagoras was a visionary and a genius; to his detractors, he was an unhinged crank and a mystical kook. Legends about him are thick on the ground – he was a strict vegetarian, some say, and he never ate beans, but he could calm a rowdy drunk just by playing a soothing melody on the pipes.

Much of this is fiction, of course. But as that last anecdote suggests, some of Pythagoras' teachings quite possibly did have to do with music. The most important musical discovery attributed to him is also one of the most contested: some say he discovered the use of mathematical ratios to describe the intervals between pitches on a scale. That is an insight that remains at the heart of music theory to this day. But in point of fact, the connection between music and maths may have become apparent more practically and less theoretically, among the craftsmen who built instruments for performance. Even so, many of Pythagoras' followers were known for their subtle and detailed speculation about the connections between music, mathematics, and the structure of the cosmos.

These Pythagorean teachings about music were extremely influential, and many of them were brought by Pythagoras' followers to Athens. Two strains of Pythagorean thought were particularly powerful: the use of mathematics to understand harmony, and the consequent attempt to connect musical sound with the laws of physics that govern planetary motion. Those ideas became part of the fast-paced intellectual environment that was developing in Athens, where scholars and self-styled experts (often called 'sophists') peddled ideas and theories about everything from biology and physics to rhetoric and politics. The sophists wanted to sell the upper classes on courses of study that could make them wise, or powerful, or both, and they did so by arguing and competing amongst themselves for the most effective and accurate ways of describing the world. The foundational philosopher Socrates, who seems to have found Pythagoreanism attractive, came of age in this fifth-century culture of debate. So did the musician Damon of Athens, who taught Pericles himself and who may have had Pythagorean ties as well. When mixed in with the bustling artistic and intellectual community that started under Peisistratus with folks like Lasus, Pythagoreanism helped kickstart a frenzy of post-Persian War debate and experimentation as performers and theorists worked to write, sing, and think about music in ever more new and compelling ways. There will be much more to say about all of this in Chapters 4, 5, and 6, because Pythagorean thought helped Athenian philosophers to make some of their most lasting contributions to world intellectual history, shaping how people all over the world would go on to think about music.

It should be clear by now that music was more than just a form of entertainment for many Greeks. It was a mystical experience and a way of life, a central part of education and a means of communicating with the divine. At dinner parties and in religious ceremonies, in school and in politics, the ancient Greeks shaped their lives around melody and rhythm. The Greek word *mousikē*, from which our 'music' eventually comes, means much more than just audible tunes. It means everything over which the Muses (*Mousai* in Greek – hence the word *mousikē*) presided. That includes dance, instrumentation, recitation, and all the forms of politics, mathematics, and religious worship which were thought to be connected with song and to have a sort of 'rhythm' and 'harmony' of their own. Still to this day, scientists and casual listeners alike are fascinated by the power of music – the ways in which it seems to activate our brainwaves and stir our emotions, maybe even connect us to God, as almost nothing else can. When we turn on Spotify or when we worship in church, we do more than just listen to sounds. We tap into something universal to our species which is at once deeply primal and profoundly sophisticated, visceral and elevated at the same time. If we have made any progress in understanding that phenomenon over the last 3,000 years, it's thanks at least in part to the revolutionary developments that happened in and around Athens, where for decades thinkers and artists from far and wide came together and wrestled with their craft as they never had before. Whether we know it or not, the way we think about and even listen to music now has been shaped by the scholars and artists of Athens and the ancient Greek world. When we come to know them better, we come to know ourselves. That is what this book is for.

Some further reading

The cultural and musical interchange between Greece and the Near East has been covered in some detail by John C. Franklin of the University of Vermont. In particular, his essay 'A Feast of Music' is very rich – it can be found in the book *Anatolian Interfaces* (Oxford: Oxbow, 2008), which in general contains some worthwhile studies of interaction between Greece and the Near East. See also 'Lyre Gods of the Bronze Age Musical Koinē' in the *Journal of Ancient Near Eastern Religions* (volume 6, number 2, 2006, pp. 39–70).

A classic treatment of the interface between Greek and Near Eastern poetic culture is Martin West's *The East Face of Helicon* (Oxford: Oxford University Press, 1997).

A book by Maarit Kivilo goes into greater detail about the biographies and careers of great Archaic poets like Terpander and Sappho. It's called *Early Greek Poets' Lives: The Shaping of the Tradition* (Leiden: Brill, 2010).

A short essay that gives a broad overview of musical life in Greece is 'Mousikē and Mimēsis' by Giulia Corrente. It can be found in *The Many Faces of Mimesis*, published in 2018 by Parnassos Press. There are two other book-length general surveys – *Music in Ancient Greece and Rome* by John G. Landels (Abingdon: Routledge, 1998) and *Music and Musicians in Ancient Greece* by Warren D. Anderson (Ithaca, NY: Cornell University Press, 1994) – which may also be useful.

For a more detailed book-length study of the topic, see Martin West's *Ancient Greek Music* (Oxford: Clarendon Press, 1992).

A much more technical and difficult, but also more up-to-date, treatment than West's is that of Stephan Hagel, *Ancient Greek Music: A New Technical History* (Cambridge: Cambridge University Press, 2009). This will be of great use to readers who wish to go deeper into detail.

Though not yet published at the time of this writing, the publishers at Blackwell will soon produce a *Companion to Ancient Greek and Roman Music* (edited by Tosca Lynch and Eleonora Rocconi). I have been fortunate enough to read some of the book in advance and can recommend it highly.

How Music Was Made: Instruments and Songs

There's more than one way to make music. There is singing, of course: singing is one of the central forms of making music pretty much anywhere music is made. And the Greeks did a lot of it. In fact, almost all of what we think of as Greek 'poetry' was actually meant to be sung in one way or another. Homer's poems, though they eventually got written down, were originally chanted from memory along a fairly simple, sing-song melody. Poets like Sappho, Alcaeus, and Timotheus are called 'lyric' poets because their poems were intended to be sung with accompaniment on the lyre. Dithyrambs, epinicians, and other choral songs were meant to be sung as well, and the great tragedians like Aeschylus and Euripides wrote words that were meant to be intoned aloud or sung. Those of us who love these poets today almost always read their work in books – we may read them in Greek or in translation, but we treat them as if they were meant to be ink on a page. In fact, though, from Homer's day all the way up through the Classical period, poetry was primarily intended to be heard, not seen.

But the Greeks also had a colourful array of different instruments – or as they called them, 'tools' (*organa*) – for producing a range of different sounds. And the choice of instrument – which tools to use, in what way, and for what purpose – was more than just an aesthetic judgement for ancient Greek artists. This is easy to understand by comparison with modern instruments: when somebody says that she studies classical piano, and has done for ten years, it's likely to elicit quite a different reaction from the one someone else will get when she says she plays electric bass in a garage band. Playing either of those instruments comes with a range of different social and cultural associations. Many people may think of the classical pianist as a dedicated, cultured aesthete. By contrast, at the mention of a bass guitarist, one might conjure up an image of ripped jeans, greasy hair, and long afternoons spent smoking substances whose names I won't mention here.

These stereotypes can be completely mistaken: plenty of people who play the electric guitar are also fluent speakers of French whose afternoons are spent in chaste reflection upon the nature of virtue. But the most prominent bass guitarists in popular culture are guys with tattoos and names like 'Flea' (from the band known as the Red Hot Chili Peppers). Whereas classical pianists tend to show up to their gigs in evening gowns or tuxedoes. And so the fact remains that, for better or for worse, different instruments come with different cultural baggage because of the way they've traditionally been used.

So, too, in ancient Greece. As we get to know the instruments which were in use during the Classical period, we'll also develop a sense of some major trends and prejudices in Athenian society. Two styles of instrument will be particularly important: strings and pipes.

Strings

We can see paintings of typical Greek stringed instruments on vase paintings like the one shown here. They were made of a hollow structure called a 'soundbox' much like the body of a guitar. Over this soundbox were stretched strings made of animal gut or sinew, which were tied to a wooden bar (called a 'yoke,' *zugon*). The bar, in turn, rested on two wooden arms (*pēcheis*, singular *pēchus*), sometimes also called 'horns' (*kerata*).

This kind of instrument is often referred to as a 'lyre' (from the Greek word *lura* – plural *lurai*). Technically, though, among the later commentators who gave each instrument an official name, the word *lura* was used to designate only one of many possible forms this instrument could take. A *lura* was perhaps the most straightforward, basic of these

Fig. 1 Terracotta amphora (vase) attributed to the Berlin Painter, featuring a kitharode with his instrument. Image courtesy of the Met Museum, New York, NY.

forms, often having a soundbox made of tortoiseshell – hence a *lura* could also be called a *chelus*, which means 'tortoise' in Greek.

One story went that the resourceful trickster god Hermes had invented the lyre out of necessity in an attempt to charm his older siblings.[1] It had a sophisticated, genteel mythological pedigree and was considered just the right kind of thing for the moneyed aristocracy to play. That's because it seemed elegant enough for the gentry, but not so elaborate and complex that it suggested an over-developed enthusiasm for music – which would have been beneath a true gentleman.

Real pros, though, played the much more elaborate *kithara* (plural *kitharai*). Eventually, that word would be adopted in Spanish as *guitarra*, which is where we get our English word 'guitar.' But the Greek *kithara*, though it shares some features with the modern guitar, was a different instrument altogether – far more ornate and elaborate, as the vase painting in Fig. 1 shows.

The *kithara* was what you played if you were serious about strings. Terpander, the legendary great whom we met in the previous chapter, played the *kithara*. So did later performers like Timotheus of Miletus in the late 400s and early 300s BC, as well as mythological heroes of music such as Orpheus, whose playing was said to have moved even stones and trees with its emotional power. The god Apollo, too, who presided over the highest forms of musical art, was often depicted wielding the *kithara* in popular portrayals.

Most *kitharai* had seven strings, but that was far from a given – those who wanted to experiment with more complicated melodies and modulations sometimes added strings on as a way of making more ornate runs of notes possible. People used to tell a story about how Terpander added more strings to his *kithara* and got scolded by Spartan authorities who wanted to keep things simple and old fashioned.[2] This is probably a tall or at least an exaggerated tale, because it's almost identical to another story that was told about Timotheus – only this time, Timotheus was supposed to have added a ninth string, and the Spartan leaders were so appalled that they demanded he cut two strings off.[3] But even though they're apocryphal, these anecdotes tell us something: musical instruments and the sounds they could or couldn't make carried huge cultural significance. Toying with the accepted makes and models could get you accused of corrupting the traditions of the ancients for the sake of flashy gimmicks.

These sorts of accusations are pretty much a constant in the history of music. When the electric guitar was invented in the 1920s and 1930s, it raised some eyebrows among traditionalists. And the acoustic guitar itself got panned as an amateur's plaything back in in the seventeenth century: 'the guitar is no more than a cowbell, so easy to play ... that there is no stable boy who is not a musician on the guitar.' So wrote the Spanish critic Sebastián de Covarrubias in a 1611 dictionary, complaining that the really substantive instrument, the lute, was being abandoned for a cheap trinket. Now, of course, acoustic guitars are perfectly respectable and even celebrated as quite appropriate for classical music by the likes of J.S. Bach and Fernando Sor – which just goes to show that these sorts of judgements are, in many cases, only a matter of time.

Similarly, different stringed instruments in ancient Greece meant different things to different generations. In the fifth century BC, the *kithara* meant showmanship and professionalism. But in earlier eras, the Homeric bards used a simpler instrument with a semi-circular soundbox, often called the *phorminx* (plural *phorminges*). Among professionals, as *phorminges* fell out of use, *kitharai*, with their square soundboxes and ornate curved arms, came more and more into vogue.

The *barbitos*, meanwhile, had more elongated strings and arms than the *kithara*, *chelus*, and *phorminx*. The *barbitos* therefore played with a deeper resonance, and it was portrayed differently than the more gentlemanly *chelus* or the more elaborate *kithara*. In myths, the *barbitos* was often placed in the hands of satyrs – rampaging goat-men with insatiable sex drives – and of those who worshipped the god of wine and chaos, Dionysus. It could therefore be connected in the public imagination to raucous partying, but it also had a history of being used by some of Greece's most celebrated musicians – I mentioned in the last chapter that Terpander himself was said to have invented the *barbitos* after hearing something similar used at a Lydian drinking party. It was said to have been favoured by Sappho, too, and other notables of the Archaic period like Alcaeus.

The *barbitos*, then, is a great example of how an instrument's connotations and cultural resonance can shift over time and depending on context. It's possible, given the myth about Terpander, that the *barbitos* came to Greece from somewhere in the East. And it may well have been a party instrument, or at least something to be played at the boozy but sophisticated social gatherings known as *symposia*, which we'll cover more in the next chapter. Those *symposia* were at once laid-back, wine-soaked affairs, and erudite, elite social gatherings. Over time, the most famous sympotic performers of one generation became the cultural legends of the next, so that what may have begun as carousing and drinking became celebrated high culture. Usually the *barbitos* was associated with eroticism of some kind, and the Greeks were never at ease with it as a staple of elite society. But in the popular consciousness, it was an instrument of many meanings – whether it was imagined in the hands of a drunken satyr, or associated with the elegant verses of Sappho, could depend upon whom you asked and when.

Pipes

Perhaps even more culturally fraught and complex in their public image were the *auloi*, the 'pipes' (singular *aulos*). This, the most popular wind instrument in ancient Greece, consisted of two pipes, played simultaneously by one musician. The pipes were often made of wood, although they could also be made of such things as bone, horn, metal, or clay. Each of the two pipes had a reed (Greek *glōssa* or *zeugos*) that would vibrate to produce sound when blown into correctly. The reed led into two sections of tubing called the *holmos* and *hypholmion*, which in turn led into the body (*bombyx*) of the pipe. This body had holes (*trēmata* or *trypēmata*) on its side which could be covered with the fingers to produce different notes.

Sometimes both *auloi* in a pair were the same length, but often one *aulos* was longer and so played lower notes than the other. Some similar instruments still exist in modern times – notably the Launeddas, a traditional Sardinian instrument consisting of three pipes. Based on studying the Launeddas and other multi-pipe instruments, some scholars (notably Armand D'Angour of Oxford) have inferred that the longer, lower-pitched *aulos* would have been used to play long, sustained notes while the other, shorter *aulos* played the melody. That's a highly plausible theory, but there are others as well, and what very little written notation we have for the *auloi* doesn't record enough specifics to tell us for sure. The two pipes may also have moved in tandem or passed the melody off from one to the other – different modern performers have tested out different theories, and the YouTube links at the end of this chapter give some examples of the variety in their work.

Vase paintings and written sources both depict *aulos*-players (auletes) with big, puffed-out cheeks a lot like the American jazz trumpeter Dizzy Gillespie. When Dizzy really got wailing, his face ballooned into a distinctive wide-eyed, round-cheeked stare that became his trademark. Auletes were known for making much the same face – probably because they practised a technique called circular breathing, which involves inhaling through the nose while still expelling air from the cheeks so the player never has to stop playing (compare the image on the cover of this book, which is Roman but includes a pipe-player with the characteristic puffed-out cheeks). Many auletes also used a leather strap called the *phorbeia* as a halter to keep the pipes in place and support the cheeks while they kept the music going.

There was a famous myth which told of how Athena, dignified goddess of wisdom and war, invented the *auloi* but then disposed of them because puffing out her cheeks to play them made her look ugly.[4] That's a classic example of how some of the more censorious critics of Greek high society in the fifth and fourth centuries BC thought of the *auloi*: crass, indecorous, and unsuitable for elite society. Even the *kithara*, which was regarded with ambivalence by those who found its professionalism troublesome, counted as more respectable than the frightfully vulgar *auloi* for such moralists as Plato, who insisted that the sound of the pipes would not even be heard in the ideal city of his *Republic*.[5]

As noted already, though, Plato is far from the whole story. In fact, in disapproving of the *auloi*, he was quite unusual – at any rate he was avowedly more concerned with his theories of how the world should be than with the realities of how it actually was. His unease, first and foremost, was with emotionalism: his student Aristotle also characterized the *auloi* as capable of expressing and inspiring tremendously profound emotions of fear, grief, ecstasy, delight, and everything in between.[6] Though Aristotle was more lax than Plato about these sorts of things, both were cautious about the intensity of feeling that *auloi* could produce: Plato worried that the theatres encouraged Athenians to hunt after pure musical enjoyment at the expense of more refined artistic pleasures, and Aristotle called pipe music 'more for parties than for edification' (the Greek word he used was *orgiastikos* – suitable for wild revelry).[7]

But behind these rather sniffy comments we can get a sense for how beloved the pipes must have been. If critics like Plato and Aristotle had to devote time and energy to running them down, *auloi* must have exerted a considerable sway over the heart and imagination of the average Athenian. We can hear that anxiety behind Aristotle's warning that pipe playing encourages an unhealthy fixation with music for the sake of music, and that it encourages irrationality (since players couldn't speak while playing the pipes, some philosophers worried that their music was devoid of the kind of sophisticated thought that came with verbal argumentation). It almost seems as if these theorists were antsy about posh young boys jamming on the pipes while they ought to be devoting themselves to serious pursuits like rhetoric and logic.

And in fact, many poets and artists – often more down-to-earth or at least more free-spirited than philosophers – celebrated the *auloi* enthusiastically for precisely those powers of expression and emotion that made Plato nervous. For instance: Telestes of Selinus, who was known for his dithyrambs and won prizes with them in the late fifth century BC, was said to have refused to believe that Athena would ever throw away such a magnificent instrument as the *auloi*.[8]

So *auloi* were not, in fact, the unremittingly lowbrow noisemakers that Plato might have liked us to believe they were. True, they were featured prominently at rowdy drinking parties, and in dithyramb, which was usually composed and performed to worship Dionysus. Like

Cybele, the mother-goddess of Phrygia whose cult made its way through Anatolia into eastern Greece, Dionysus was often honoured with frenzied dancing and ecstatic music on the pipes. But the powerful feelings inspired by *aulos* music were also employed to great effect at all levels of Greek society: in the high art of tragedy, for example, in sombre rituals such as funerals, and at sporting events. The compelling emotional tenor and versatility of the *auloi*, so threatening to the imagined world order of utopian theorists, was likely also exactly what made them such a welcome accompaniment in the lively day-to-day of actual Athens.

In fact, though, it's hard to be certain what the 'average bloke' would have thought, because it was the rarefied gentry who wrote things down. That's a problem with any study of ancient history – or modern history, for that matter. The further back one goes in time, the higher percentage chance there is that the lower classes won't have had the resources or the education to write or read extensively. A large portion of what survives from ancient Athens – whether it be pro-*aulos*, anti-*aulos*, or anything in between – is quite specialized and erudite scholarly commentary meant to be shared among small circles within the upper crust.

Granted, those circles contained very influential people, and by and large the writers of the Greek gentry were not trying to deceive their readers: they were representing and discussing the attitudes of the citizenry, and especially the upper classes, as they saw them. But what we don't get from such sources is a really fine-grained sense of how slaves, or the uneducated, or even most women of any social class, would have thought about music. It's important to keep that in mind: whenever we think about the ancient world, we're only getting part of the picture. It's especially a problem with respect to music, which often lives and breathes among the common folks and not the upper crust. The snobbery directed at the *auloi* in our extant sources definitely reflects a real cultural attitude, but it almost certainly muffles the immense excitement and energy with which auletes would have been met by their crowds of adoring fans.

After all, there were competitions in *aulos*-playing all over Greece, and there's no indication that they went over less well than the *kithara* contests. Dithyrambic contests were featured in the Great Dionysia, the yearly festival where tragedies were performed in Athens, in the illustrious Panathenaia, and in a number of other smaller festivals on the outskirts of town. As mentioned already, these festivals were massive civic events packed with people from all over the city and its suburbs – the energy at them must have been electrifying. Not even the most disdainful critic was able to stop the electric or acoustic guitar from catching on in its day – the *auloi* were no different.

The real thing

Our information about how pipes and strings were perceived comes from written sources – poets and critics commenting on how they saw the world of musical culture. Some of our knowledge about how the instruments themselves were constructed comes from imagery like the ones painted on vases which we saw earlier in this chapter. But we have another source of information when it comes to ancient instruments: we have the real things. No *kitharai* have yet been found, but archaeologists have uncovered some battered remains of *auloi* which help tell us a lot about how things worked.

One of the most important surviving pipes is the 'Louvre Aulos,' so called because it can now be found at the Louvre museum in Paris (listed under inventory number E10962). No one knows exactly how old it is, but it likely is Egyptian and comes from a community of ancient Greeks who lived in that part of the world and brought much of their cultural practice with them. The pipes are marvellously, improbably well-preserved – they are made of an African wood which the Greeks called *lōtos*, meaning that by all accounts they shouldn't have survived as well as they have. It's hugely helpful that they did, because one of the many things they let us do is confirm our understanding of the Greek scale. By measuring the distance between finger-holes, scholars can determine which notes the instrument is designed to play, and calculate the intervals which would have been available to auletes working with a pipe like this one.

It turns out that the scale played by the Louvre Aulos spans an octave and plus a fourth, and the notes available are those of what theorists called the 'Greater Perfect System.' This is a technical name for a sequence of notes, centred around an octave scale, which theorists used as something like the basic outline of a standard scale. This theory will be covered in more detail in Chapter 7. For now it suffices to say that the Greater Perfect System was structured in a way not unlike our modern Western scale, but including some smaller intervals (that is, some notes closer together in pitch) than most of our modern instruments are capable of playing.

By stopping up different holes with his fingers, an aulete could shorten the column of air vibrating inside the pipe just the way recorder-players do with their instruments. A shorter column means a higher note, so fingering one's way along the pipe meant walking up the scale. But there was more that an aulete could do than just play a basic scale, of course. By covering the holes only partially, or by adjusting the positioning of his mouth on the reed (a technique called 'embouchure' in modern terminology), the player could bend the pitch up and down. This allowed for the delicate shifts in pitch that would distinguish between the different 'shades' or types of scale known as chromatic, enharmonic, and diatonic (more on these, too, in Chapter 7). Players could also 'overblow' (a blowing technique which produces higher pitches than the basic ones normally available to the instrument), and they could keep some holes permanently plugged with wax, especially if their pipes had more holes than their hands had fingers (i.e. more than five – the Louvre *aulos* pipes, for example, have seven and nine holes, respectively). For a more technologically advanced solution, a device called a 'collar' (Greek *syrinx*) could be used to close off certain holes without the use of fingers, freeing up the hands and giving access to a greater number of notes.

The Louvre Aulos isn't the only one to survive. The one pictured here is housed at Reading University – it's made of wood, but covered with bronze and decorated with silver, giving an example of how variable the

Fig. 2 An *aulos*, of uncertain provenance, housed at the University of Reading. Wood covered in bronze with silver decoration. Voluremuseum, Wikimedia Commons. Cropped. https://creativecommons.org/licenses/by-sa/4.0/deed.en.

construction of the instruments could be. Another set of pipes was uncovered in 1996 within a fourth-century BC tomb in the Macedonian port city of Pydna, on the northwestern coast of the Aegean Sea. Using these ancient remains as guides, some creative scholars have ventured into making reconstructed models, often going to great lengths to obtain authentic materials. One such scholar-artist, Barnaby Brown, has had deer knucklebones flown in from Scotland and stripped of flesh using acid to recreate the *holmos* as closely as possible. Barnaby's adventures, and those of his colleagues, are described on the Workshop of Dionysus blog (see the url below).

This is an excellent example of how texts, archaeological study, and practical experience can reinforce one another. The study of ancient music is dynamic, and it challenges researchers to think outside the box. Because so much of music is a felt thing and only imperfectly captured in words, scholars can't simply read theory to understand how it works. They also have to get their hands on what they can by way of practical materials, exploring and experimenting with the kinds of sounds it's possible to make. The traditional methods of studying the ancient world – combing through written texts, for example, and digging up physical remains – have to be combined with more creative and artistic work, to check theory against a felt sense of musical artistry (and vice versa).

Strike up the band

Auloi aren't the only kinds of instruments that have been discovered. In 1981, in the Athenian district of Daphne, a fifth-century BC gravesite was revealed to house a musician and some fragmentary shards of his harp. The Greek harp (*psaltērion*) may originally have come from Lydia, although there are a number of examples preserved in Egypt. It was a triangular wooden frame with many more strings than the *kithara* (some of the Egyptian instruments have twenty-one altogether). Vase paintings and written sources show that there were all kinds of harps in ancient Greece, but none of them was considered quintessentially 'Greek' – whether from Lydia or elsewhere, the harp had an air of 'foreignness' about it. Our evidence is a little too scarce, though, to say much more than that.

There was also a range of wind instruments beyond the *auloi*, the best known of which is probably the *syrinx*. A *syrinx* was a row of reed pipes aligned next to one another in order of increasing length. This was a simple instrument, first used by shepherds in the 2000s BC on the Cycladic islands southeast of mainland Greece. Cycladic culture is ancient even by Greek standards, and in the urbane society of Classical Athens the *syrinx* pipe seemed like a quaint holdover from a simpler time. Some people refer to the *syrinx* by the name of 'pan-pipes,' because of the ancient myth of its original creation. The story went that Syrinx was once the name of a beautiful young woodland spirit, a nymph, who vowed that she would never marry or make love. The lusty god Pan – half goat, half human, and always on the prowl – tried to force himself on Syrinx. When she prayed for deliverance, Zeus turned her into the marshy reeds which Pan used to make the first pan-pipes.[9]

There were percussion instruments, too: cymbals (Greek *kymbala*), tambourines (*tympana*), and a large kind of castanet held in the hand and clapped together (the *krotala*). Eventually (in the third century BC), an adventurous inventor named Ctesibius, working in the bustling intellectual hub of Egypt's Alexandria, even invented something like an organ, the *hydraulis*. By manipulating air and water pressure using a sophisticated system of levers, *hydraulis* players could force air through a series of pipes to generate a powerful, piercing sound.[10] And there were plenty of other musical contraptions besides, many of which don't survive at all except for their names. The *aulos* and the *kithara* were always at the centre of the Greek musical world, but around them was arrayed a whole orchestra of backup instruments for various occasions, each with its own specific history, legends, and cultural connotations.

And they came from all over the place. The *barbitos* and the harp may have come from Lydia or perhaps Egypt. Most Greek historians and poets considered the *aulos* to have been invented in Phrygia, another district of Asia Minor. Whether or not these attributions are exactly correct, they testify to an awareness among ancient Greek musicians that they shared a common heritage with the artists of the Near East. In fact, there was probably a great deal of back-and-forth cultural exchange going on throughout the 1000s BC, resulting not only in the adoption of Eastern instruments by Greek players but the reverse as well – an outwards exportation of Greek models into the East and beyond.

World music

Greece and Mesopotamia certainly shared one crucially important instrumental practice: they ordered their strings in the same way.

In modern music, we think of the most important note in a scale (the 'tonic') as the bottom note: that's the note around which a traditionally harmonized song will gravitate and to which it will probably return by the end of its melody. In Greek music, though, this central note really was *central*: it was the one played on the middle of the *kithara*'s seven strings. Hence it was called not the 'tonic' but the *mesē*, a Greek word meaning 'middle.'

The other notes in the scale were named and tuned according to their relationship with that central note. In the modern system, scale notes have names and functions beginning from the tonic and walking upwards: after the tonic (1st) come the supertonic (2nd), the mediant (3rd), the subdominant (4th), the dominant (5th), the submediant (6th), and the leading tone (7th), each with its own particular role to play in the melody. Greek had an analogous set of names for the notes of its scale: the seven central notes of the scale are called *hypatē*, *parhypatē*, *lichanos*, *mesē*, *paramesē*, *paranētē*, and *nētē*. These names refer to the physical position of each string on the instrument: *hypatē* ('highest') is the string which would have been highest above *mesē* in a standard lyre, while *nētē* ('lowest') would have been lowest beneath it. Somewhat confusingly, the notes themselves actually went from high to low in pitch as the strings went from low to high. Like a guitar, a lyre was normally held horizontally with its lowest-sounding string highest up: so *hypatē*, for instance, was called 'highest' because it was played on the string positioned highest on the instrument, but in fact it was the *lowest* note of the scale in pitch. Similarly, *nētē* was the highest note, and so on.

This distinctive method of tuning is the same one implied by the oldest written tune in known existence, mentioned at the very beginning of this book. These 'Hurrian hymns' come from the Levantine town of Ugarit in what is now Syria. The notation of the hymns assigns a role to each note according to which string would have played it and its relation to the *middle* string – just like the Greek system. This is how we know that Greeks and Syrians were tuning their instruments in the same way as early as the 1400s BC. That particular practice probably made its way into the Aegean from Mesopotamia in a trend known as 'East-West cultural drift.' But the exchange also went the other way from time to time. For example, sculptures and reliefs from the Levant often depict the use of a *kinnāru*, an Eastern stringed instrument with a distinctive flat base. But eventually, cultures in Levantine cities such as Ashdod seem to have adopted a round-based lyre, which can only have come from the early Greek cultures in the Aegean. This might have happened around 1200 BC, when the great Mycenaean palaces of the Late Bronze Age seem to have collapsed and sent the nobility of the Greek islands eastwards to places like Ashdod. The *kithara* and the *aulos* were distinctively Greek instruments, but they were both known to have taken shape long before the fifth century in dialogue with other cultures from around the world.

Greek instruments also outlasted both Athens and the fifth century. We've already noted one distant echo of the *kithara* that still survives today: our word 'guitar,' which is derived from the Greek word through French and Spanish. This small linguistic tribute bears witness to the fact that when early modern musicians in Europe developed their own tradition of stringed instrumentation, they did so in a tradition that went back to ancient Greece.

But the *aulos* lasted too, especially in Italy. In fact, the image on this book's cover, though it depicts a distinctly Greek-looking set of pipes, is from a Roman sculpture on one of Rome's major roads, the *Via Appia*. The Latin word for *aulos* is *tibia* (plural *tibiae*), and it was among the most popular instruments in Rome.

For example, in Pompeii, the volcanic eruption of Mount Vesuvius froze an entire city in time in 79 AD. The ash of Vesuvius hardened and caked over the remains of countless artefacts from daily life – including four complete *tibia* pipes. These pipes are technically elaborate and certainly made for professional use – some of them have as many as fifteen finger-holes. So players would certainly have used rotating collars in addition to their fingers to manipulate the pitch. But at heart, the Pompeii *tibiae* are basically Greek: they follow much the same model as Greek *auloi*, and their holes are spaced to play the scales developed by Greek theory.

Much of the Athenian musical tradition would probably have been handed on to the Roman Empire by Greek slaves and emigrants. But Roman conquerors would have also found some Greek pipes ready-made in Italy as they travelled across the peninsula. Just north of Naples in Poseidonia (now Paestum), for example, archaeologists have unearthed a pair of pipes from around 480 BC, about 200 years before the Romans took over.

Poseidonia was one of many Greek colonies in Southern Italy, and since about the sixth century BC it had been occupied by settlers as part of what is called Magna Graecia (Latin for 'Big Greece') – a swath of

Italian land where adventurous Greeks in the Archaic period often landed after setting out from their original homes in search of wider territory. Magna Graecia became a place where the customs and traditions of Greek culture were partially exported into what would eventually become Roman territory. During the Classical period, as Greek ideas and art continued to make their way westward, musical practices were also swept up in this tide of trade between the original Greece and her offshoot colonies. That meant that when the Romans took over in the Hellenistic period, they found Greek music – and instruments like the *auloi* – waiting for them to make their own.

All of this raises an interesting question: what is Greek music anyway? If the instruments that Athens loved came at least in part from Egypt and the Levant, and if they found their way far out beyond the borders of the city as time went on, was there even anything about it that was distinctly Greek, let alone Athenian?

To some extent, the answer is simple: Athenian music was Athenian because it was performed in Athens. Much of what we know about ancient music comes from sources outside of the city. But because Athens set itself up as *the* place to be in the Mediterranean for arts and culture during the fifth century, it became a site where crucial interchange and development happened that made Greek instruments – and the songs they played – visible for posterity. The thought of Lasus and Damon, the songs of Timotheus and Euripides – these have connections and origins in places all over the world, but it was in Athens that they bumped up against one another and made their most enduring marks on cultural history. Even those artists and thinkers from this period whose work doesn't survive in written form did much to shape that of others who did leave written records.

And so being a nexus of social and intellectual interaction didn't just make Athens into a hodgepodge grab-bag of random people and musical ideas. Athens in the fifth century was a hothouse, where musical practice and theory rubbed against one another to make something distinctive and new. The radical tunings developed in the late 400s BC, the alterations and additions to the structure of *kitharai* and *auloi* that corresponded to those developments, and the fractious debate within urbane Athenian society about how those changes ought to be regarded, endorsed, or forbidden: all of these together made up a magnetically attractive local culture which has fascinated and influenced later musicians ever since.

The Roman poet Horace, who lived in the first century BC under the reign of Julius Caesar's heir, Augustus, wrote in one of his poems that 'conquered Greece conquered her savage captor.'[11] By this he meant that even though Rome became politically dominant, the cultural practices of Greece and especially Athens were so mesmerizing that Roman high society became fixated on and addicted to Greek ways of life. The Romans weren't the only ones. Melodies, tuning practices, and instruments from Greece endured long past their respective heydays and changed the game in all sorts of ways, not least when it came to the strings and the double-pipes. From their origins in the Cyclades and Lydia, to their transformative ascendancy in Classical Athens, to their dissemination to the Roman Empire and around the world, Greek music made itself heard long after its instruments fell silent.

Some further reading

There are plenty of images, videos, and how-to's concerning the reconstruction of ancient instruments (*auloi* especially) on the 'Workshop of Dionysus' blog: http://www.doublepipes.info/.

Volume I of Andrew Barker's *Greek Musical Writings* (Cambridge: Cambridge University Press, 1984, subtitled *The Musician and His Art*) contains some very helpful diagrams, explanations, and illustrations of Greek instruments in the introduction. So does Martin West's classic *Ancient Greek Music* (Oxford: Clarendon Press, 1992). Also useful for stringed instruments is *Stringed Instruments of Ancient Greece* by Martha Maas and Jane McIntosh Snyder (New Haven, CT: Yale University Press, 1989).

The politics and symbolism attached to different Greek instruments is an issue that has attracted a lot of scholarly attention – two central treatments are 'The Politics of the New Music' by Eric Csapo (in *Music and the Muses*, edited by Penelope Murray and Peter Wilson, Oxford: Oxford University Press, 2004, pp. 207–48) and Timothy Powers's *The Culture of Kitharoidia* (Cambridge, MA: Harvard University Press, 2010).

Also enjoyable and informative is Robert R. Wallace's 'An Early Fifth-Century Athenian Revolution in Aulos Music' in *Harvard Studies in Classical Philology* (volume 101, 2003, pp. 73–92).

John Franklin will cover the instrumental exchange between East and West in his contribution to Blackwell's *Companion to Ancient Greek and Roman Music*.

For those interested in learning more about the *hydraulis* (and the history of organs more generally), there's a very detailed diagram and explanation in 'Early History of the Organ' by Willi Apel in the journal *Speculum* (volume 23, number 2, 1984, pp. 191–216). In 2002, Dr. Richard Pettigrew of the University of Oregon gave a detailed interview on the topic, which can be found at this link: https://www.archaeologychannel.org/audio-main-menu-cat/audio-interviews/307-about-the-ancient-hydraulis.

Where Music Happened: Venues

Music doesn't just come out of nowhere. Songs aren't abstractions: they don't exist in some airy space above the earth and outside of time. Sometimes, in the modern world, we can get used to thinking about songs and compositions as if they were immutable, eternal ideas. When we write music down using notation, we create the misleading impression that it can be perfectly reproduced. Now that J. S. Bach's 'Magnificat in D Major' or Lil Nas X's 'Old Town Road' exist on paper, it seems like they can be performed the same way over and over again, communicated across time and space. This lets us fall into the assumption that each song exists in some perfect, Platonic form to be plucked out of the air anytime and anywhere.

But in fact, context matters. A quick search for 'Ode to Joy Flashmob' on YouTube returns a long list of videos in which classically trained performers bring their instruments to unexpected places – from an office skyscraper in Minneapolis, to a public square in Nürnberg – and surprise passers-by with a performance of Beethoven's masterwork. The whole point of the exercize is that a new location makes the experience quite different from a more traditional performance of the same piece in a concert hall. When the artists are in casual clothing, pretending to be part of the crowd until the last minute, they create a brand new kind of art that looks and indeed sounds different than other versions.

Things get still more shocking when an artist puts a song somewhere it was never meant to go – as, for example, in Stanley Kubrick's film adaptation of the novel *A Clockwork Orange*. There, the soaring orchestration of 'Ode to Joy' is played alongside horrific scenes of violence so that watching and listening creates a sense of surprise and revulsion rather than exultation. Audience, location, and artistic intentions can influence artists' emphases and interpretation in performance. Where, when, and why you play a song changes how the song comes across – even if the notes on the page would look exactly the same each time.

This was still more true in the ancient world. Because though the Greeks did develop notation, and though that notation has been crucial for us in partially recovering their music, it wasn't their primary way of learning or thinking about songs. A song in fifth-century BC Athens wasn't ink on a page or an abstract idea in somebody's head: it was a particular event, a performance in time and space that occurred once and once only. It wasn't 'Aeschylus' *Persians*' in general: it was a glitzy production of a never-before-seen tragedy in front of a huge crowd. It wasn't 'Pindar's *Pythian Ode* 1': it was a concert performance for a live audience at a king's victory celebration. Each of those events was unique, and often – as in the case of tragedy – not likely to be repeated any time soon. It's worth spending some time, therefore, thinking about where the Greeks liked to play their music, and how their venues shaped their songs.

Some of those venues were made for music, and some weren't. In a moment, we'll survey the official concert spaces of ancient Greece – buildings and structures made specially to house musical performance. But probably the majority of singing, dancing, and playing didn't happen in fancy stone theatres or on wooden stage platforms. Most music is performed in what scholars call 'occasional' settings – places whose primary purpose is something other than music.

Whistle while you work

If you take stock of the music in your own life, you are likely to find that a quite small percentage of the songs you listen to are actually performed in a concert setting where the music is the main event. The vast majority of musical consumption these days doesn't happen that way for most people. Perhaps the most memorable musical experiences of life do tend to take place in spaces specifically designed for music. But most day-to-day music listening happens in the car, or while typing away at a computer, or in the background at parties.

Something similar could be said of ancient Greek life, and in fact parties were among the most important contexts where music was learned, tested, and enjoyed. An ancient Greek dinner party was called a *symposium* (plural *symposia*). The word literally means 'drinking together,' but though the booze was plentiful it was far from the only focus of the party. These were intimate but lively affairs involving only men – guests gathered in the *andrōn* ('men's chambers'), a room of the host's house where no women were allowed. Or rather, no *free* women were allowed – female slaves and prostitutes, on the other hand, were rarely absent.

In fact, they were often the ones making the music. A standard *symposium* would include a slave-girl with instructions to play *aulos* music, either in the background or at the centre of attention when a diversion was needed. The philosopher Plato wrote a fictional account of one fifth-century *symposium* in which the great sage Socrates conducted an inquiry into the nature of love. At the beginning of that dialogue, the host leads a female slave in to accompany the festivities with *aulos* music as a matter of course. When one of the guests asks the girl to leave, that's considered remarkable – an unusual sign of seriousness which sets this more sober gathering apart from most parties.[1] The girl is sent to play in another room (the *gunaikeia* or women's chambers), where the women are housed.

This is a feature of life in ancient Athens which seems deeply alien, and pretty unpalatable, to most modern Europeans and Americans: the simple fact of the matter is, fifth-century Athenian life involved a lot of gender segregation. Women were allowed only into certain spaces, and as a result they could only play and hear certain kinds of music. The vast range of instruments and performance styles that we surveyed in the last chapter was not open to everyone. If you weren't a man, you weren't likely to be trained for concert performance on the *kithara*, for example.

Upper-class women had a specific type of instrument, the cradle *kithara* (so named because its soundbox was rounded on the bottom like a cradle) reserved for them – its gentle tones were considered appropriate for matrons at their looms. Slave-girls, on the other hand, could play the sultry pipes sometimes associated with theatre music and raucous dancing. So class comes into this, too: the lifestyle reserved for women was often actually reserved for *noble* women – different places and activities were permitted to other, less fortunate girls.

This isn't the place to resolve all the anxieties and discomforts that these facts may raize. In such a short book, the best that can be said is this: studying the ancient world means grappling with the fact that social mores change. They change radically over time – so radically that societies to which we owe a great deal may come to look impossibly backwards to us even as we study them to learn their wisdom. Still more unnervingly, it may be that some of our own practices, apparently unobjectionable to us now, will look barbaric to our descendants. We can't escape this complexity either by condemning the past wholesale (which would mean losing access to all that was great about antiquity as well) or by considering ourselves morally superior in every way (which will turn out to be false in the long run). Nevertheless, it's worth pausing to note, as we study the ancient Athenians, that we can learn from them without slavishly emulating or approving of them. Their ways were not our ways.

But some things never seem to change, and one of them is this: rowdy drinkers love to sing rowdy songs. It wasn't just slave-girls that made music at *symposia*: elite male guests gave impromptu performances as well. Think party playlist meets open-mic night: it wasn't uncommon for the host to invite a tune or composition from everyone in the circle of drinkers. And the *symposium*'s wilder cousin, the *kōmos* – a kind of bar crawl mixed with a parade – featured young men running late at night through the streets of the city, singing and playing on the *barbitos*.

It may well be that some of the songs which come down to us from the Archaic and Classical periods got their start as drinking tunes. We learned in Chapter 1 about the famous lyric melodies of Sappho and Terpander – we can add to these names that of Anacreon, a sixth-century lyricist known for his drinking songs and hymns. 'Let us hang garlands of celery across our foreheads and call a festival to Dionysus!' is one example of a typical Anacreontic call to celebration. Others invite listeners to go out and find love, or bewail the cold sweats that come over a young buck confronted with his crush. These are rousing lyrics meant to celebrate the vigour of life and probably to invite thunderous approval from a tipsy crowd – we may imagine people roaring out the last lines in unison, calling for another round.

But not everyone can be an Anacreon – plenty of sophisticated men had little or no skill at original composition, but were still called upon to contribute a line or two at parties. Images of *symposia* like the one shown here, painted on the wall in the 'Tomb of the Diver' (an archaeological discovery from the fifth century BC in the Greek colony of Poseidonia) suggest that music-making could be done casually by guests while drinking and perhaps even other conversation was still going on. For those without a knack for writing new songs, there was a

Fig. 3 A fresco painting of guests at a symposium, one holding a stringed instrument. Carole Raddato, Wikimedia Commons. https://creativecommons.org/licenses/by-sa/2.0/deed.en.

plentiful canon of classics by the greats to pull from. Accounts like the *Symposium* of Xenophon bear witness to a culture of quotation and re-performance in which drinkers could borrow old favourites and even alter them – whether intentionally or by a failing of memory – for the occasion.[2]

This is a good example of how professional and amateur musicianship can influence one another reciprocally. Think of the way in which some musical forms – HAUS and Electronica, for instance – were shaped in their origins by improvisational practice at informal get-togethers. Hip-hop, too, got its start on the streets of the Bronx where kids would gather to pass the time. The music took on its distinctive sound by catering to the needs of a block party, before later getting picked up by big record labels and commercialized for a wider audience. Then, when those records really got big, people all over the USA and the world started to dance and sing in ways inspired by hip-hop. Casual party music changed the industry game, and then the industry fed its way back into the ground-level culture. A similar sort of dynamic seems to have been part of the music scene in Athens: professional concert compositions would often mimic or evoke the atmosphere of casual *symposia* and private get-togethers, while private get-togethers in turn featured and repurposed some of the biggest hits and classics.

Plenty of other activities in Greece came with background music, too. Aristides Quintilianus tells us that manual labourers and their bosses would sometimes have pipe players accompany them to help lessen the tedium and discomfort of their work – this may represent a later practice from provinces controlled by the Roman Empire, but it's perfectly easy to imagine it happening in classical Athens as well.[3] Certainly, in the Classical period and even before, soldiers used trumpets and pipes to rouse their spirits and give tactical signals that could be heard on a crowded battlefield – think of modern equivalents like Taps and Reveille, the trumpet melodies used to mourn or waken American soldiers.[4] Greeks at all levels of society tended to agree that music could make pretty much anything better, and then as now the right song at the right time could create the perfect mood for almost any occasion.

The music of the gods

There was one occasion, in particular, where music was a must: so far as we know, no religious or ceremonial procession was complete without singing and dancing. We're on especially difficult ground here because religious rites are even more shrouded in mystery than most Athenian social practices. Some of the most important traditions were purposefully kept secret – such as, for example, the biannual celebrations at Eleusis (about fourteen miles west of Athens), where a select group of initiates would honour the goddess of grain and harvest, Demeter, and her daughter, Persephone.

Our descriptions of the mysteries are often hostile (as in the case of later Christian writers) or comedic (as in the case of that great entertainer, the fifth-century Athenian playwright Aristophanes). But all include singing and dancing as part of the solemn procession from Athens to Eleusis. 'Keep quiet and stand aside, out of the way of our dancing,' proclaim the choral celebrants in Aristophanes' spoofed version of the Mysteries: 'anyone who never watched the revelry of the Muses and never danced – keep away!'⁵ The origin story of Demeter's worship at Eleusis is itself recorded in a hymn – the *Homeric Hymn to Demeter*, written and performed after the *Iliad* and *Odyssey*, but somewhat in the style of a miniature Homeric epic. Though the details are hazy, it's clear music was an essential aspect of Demeter's worship.

There would have been other public processions involving religious music – pretty much any time a god was being celebrated, the *auloi* and/ or the *kithara* were involved. Weddings, too, occasioned singing in the street. Bride and groom would walk through the city accompanied by wedding songs (*hymenaia*), and guests would even stand outside the bridal chamber to sing special consummation songs (*epithalamia*) while the couple spent their first night together.

When we think about music in modern religious festivals today – in churches, synagogues, and mosques, for example – we often think about pre-prepared songs learned in advance by a select choir, or pre-written hymns that everyone in the congregation is invited to sing in the same

way each time. There was pre-prepared singing in Greek worship, too –
we certainly have the text of hymns and choral songs from the Archaic
period onwards, many of which seem to have been performed at major
temple celebrations. But there may have been some more ribald
improvisation as well. Some of the hymns were stately and used the
high-flown diction of Homeric gods and heroes. But others were more
lowbrow and came in the call-and-response form of popular song
(Aristophanes gives us a few parodies of wedding song that seem to be
based on this boisterous model).[6]

But there was another religious festival where the music was well-
rehearsed, and that was the City Dionysia which took place every year
around the month we call March.

It's possible that the Dionysia began as an occasional setting for
music. Aristotle, at least, reports that the historical roots of the Dionysia
were to be found in dithyrambic processions – choral dances and songs
in honour of the god Dionysus.[7] Before Peisistratus' reign and the
transformation of festival culture which accompanied it, the story goes
that cultic groups would stage regular but more free-form dances and
processions as a way of celebrating the god of wine and madness. It
wasn't until later that the festival got a regular date and a stable venue –
the Theatre of Dionysus, carved into the side of the hill on which Athens'
major citadel, the Acropolis, rested. If this is correct, then it's a good
example of how popular performance can form the basis for a more
stable, professionalized venue – that is, of how *occasional* performance
can give rise to *architectural* spaces specifically designated for the
enjoyment and creation of musical culture.

Music on the stage

But there's a problem, which is that Aristotle lived much later than
Peisistratus and might not have known any better than we do where the
Dionysia actually came from. What does seem clear is that this massive
festival included elements of popular performance – every ceremony

began with a procession outside the walls of the city, for example – but formalized them into a much more polished and produced event, complete with architectural stability and public subsidy. The Theatre of Dionysus was among the most famous examples of a Greek theatre – a distinctive rounded stage surrounded by a semicircle of seats whose dimensions were expertly calibrated to perfect the acoustics.

Before amps and speakers – before iPod earbuds, surround sound, soundproofing, or car stereos – the Greek theatre was among the great achievements of acoustic technology. Using the natural slope of a hillside as their starting material, architects carved out a hollow half-sphere, or *koilon*, into which they would set the audience's seats. In Athens, these were made of disposable wood throughout most of the fifth century, although by the fourth they had been replaced with stone seating banks, some of which can still be seen today. The seats sloped down until they hit a round, flat stage platform called the *orchēstra*, where the chorus would dance. (The name is Greek for 'dancing space', and it's the origin of our modern word 'orchestra' – in a modern theatre, the orchestra sits right in front of the seats, roughly where the Greek orchestra would have been).

Greek tragic theatres had two entrances to the right and left (the *parodoi*) along which actors could enter and exit, and some later designs also included a raized wooden platform (a *bēma*) for the main actors. But the most important feature of all this for our purposes is what the whole structure did to sound. Because of the rounded curve of the *koilon* and the sloped descent of the seats, words and songs from the stage were amplified enormously so that even the audience in the very back of the crowd could hear – once the seats were made of stone, they even served as dampeners to filter out low-frequency sounds and let the performers' higher-pitched voices pierce through. All these effects remain powerful in the Greek theatres that still survive: listening to someone speak on a Greek stage leaves little doubt that this is the work of a culture with a collective passion for sound quality.

This meant that, however chaotic the opening procession may have been, attendees at the City Dionysia could probably hear the main event with considerable precision. That main event, of course, was tragedy – one of the enduring achievements of Greek literary and musical culture. Tragedies were a bit like operettas: many of the words which we usually read on a page or hear spoken aloud onstage today were actually sung and chanted in an elaborate musical style. Choral songs would have been accompanied with intricate dancing and *aulos*-music, and actors playing the main roles would regularly engage members of the chorus in a back-and-forth exchange of sung lines (this kind of lyric dialogue was called an *amoibaion*). Audience members piled into their seats for long hours at a time, watching three tragedians present their newest work in hopes of winning the grand prize.

The plays came in threes – each poet would present a trilogy, often one that followed a single mythological narrative. At the end, for some light relief, there followed a 'satyr play' in which actors dressed up as mythological goat-men and bumbled their way through a ribald comedy – perhaps a spoofed version of the serious narrative that had just been shown, or a farcical mock-up of some other famous story. The subject matter was incredibly varied, but the style – elevated, stately language for the tragedy and lowbrow antics for the satyr plays – was consistent throughout, making the genre as a whole extremely distinctive and recognisable.

The same is almost certainly true of the music, although so little of it survives: tragedians would have composed their songs with a distinctive personal flair (Euripides, for example, was famous for playing around with daring new stylistic and rhythmic twists, whereas Aeschylus was said to be grave and spare in his compositional choices). But they all would have stayed mostly within the conventions of the genre. Those conventions certainly involved rhythm – some standard rhythms of tragic music are covered in Chapter 8 – and probably also involved some rules about melody (in Chapter 5, we'll see that tonal correspondence between spoken and sung language was a hallmark of traditional Greek music). Looking at our small fragment of surviving written music from Euripides' *Orestes* (featured in Chapter 7), we can discern an eerie, unsettled anxiety expressed through the frenetic rhythms and creeping quarter-tone melody. This was probably a mainstay of tragic music. But there were surely other regular tragic styles, as well – regal fanfares to go with the arrival of kings onstage, for example, or keening dirges to accompany the lamentation of bereaved wives.

There were other forms of theatre at other Athenian festivals, too. The Lenaea, held in the winter, was a smaller celebration of the same god, Dionysus, who also presided over the larger Dionysia. There, comedy was presented in much the same fashion as tragedy. In this case, as with tragedy, the performances may have evolved from a more casual, *ad hoc* presentation into something more formalized and quasi-professional. The comedies, of which only Aristophanes' survive in full, would have come with their own style of music. Usually, it's fair to assume that comedic music would have been much more zany than that of tragedy, to go with the broad and bawdy humour of the plays.

On the other hand, though, there are parodies of tragic music in some of Aristophanes' plays, and those would likely have been performed in a more lugubrious (albeit exaggerated) style.[8] In general, since Athenian comedy lampooned all aspects of Athenian public life, there are points at which it would have contained joke versions of hymns, dithyrambic song and dance, wedding songs, and much more – the music of comedy would have been among the most stylistically variable music around. None of Aristophanes' tunes survive, but what do survive are his many jokes *about* music, some of which will appear in the pages of this book. Since he was (broadly speaking) a cultural conservative, Aristophanes critiqued the music he heard around him from a very definite point of view: the old, traditional, simple songs were the best ones, he thought, and the complicated riffs of innovators like Euripides were to be shunned and mocked. This bias – plus a hefty penchant for the absurd – means we have to take Aristophanes' comments with a grain of salt. But if treated with caution, comedy can tell us quite a bit about how musical tastes evolved in Athens over the course of its fifth-century cultural explosion.

There are two important points about musical institutions in Athens that we can extract from this quick survey of dramatic festivals. First, Athenian music, even when fairly stylized and formal, was a community endeavour. Tragedians were professionals, but they directed their own plays and were given amateur actors for their choruses taken from the ranks of elite citizen males. Their art likely grew in some fashion out of local practices and only became professionalized in stages, slowly developing into a fixed art with advanced architectural technology and financial backing to support it.

Second, the people we think of as Athenian 'poets' were, more often than not, Athenian *composers*. This is worth stressing once again, especially in relation to the tragedians: Aeschylus and Euripides didn't only write 'words,' or what we would think of today as 'poems.' They composed *songs*, and they conceived of those songs in a specific time and place, woven into a particular cultural fabric and performed at a particular venue. The vast majority of Greek tragedies got one full performance and one only, the City Dionysia at which they were originally shown. So playwrights, much like other composers such as the lyricists and the competitive instrumentalists whom we've already met, would have fashioned their creations with a specific context and setting in mind. The cultural institutions of Athens shaped the kinds of music that accompanied them, just as the music itself did much to create the character of the institutions. The two were tightly bound in a reciprocal and mutually productive relationship.

Old material in new venues

That's not to say that tragedy, just like lyric, didn't find its way into other places than its original venue. Schoolchildren might memorize portions of famous plays in their lessons. Partygoers might recite a speech or a few lines to impress their friends – indeed, tragedians (such as the young wunderkind Agathon) were often guests of honour at *symposia*. And in later centuries there were concert performances featuring excerpts of old favourites (we have one papyrus which seems to come from such a performance featuring sections from Euripides' *Iphigenia at Aulis*).[9] A few truly iconic plays were even granted the rare honour of a re-performance during the author's lifetime (Aeschylus' *Persians*, for example, got an on-the-road reprize in Sicily). But these were secondary usages of material that was intended for a different context entirely – like a botanist transposing a foreign plant into a new, hothouse environment.

There's a sense in which our modern readings and performances of Greek poetry and tragedy are themselves versions of this same practice: we take art that was meant for one place and time, and we relocate it into a modern classroom or theatre. This raizes the question: how valid is that kind of exercize, if at all? Since music in ancient Athens was composed with a specific setting in mind, and since any alteration of that setting turns the original performance into something new, haven't we lost what's essential about Greek music irrevocably? With all this distance of time and space between us and ancient Greece, isn't it hopeless to think we could ever recover the real thing?

If the 'real thing' is the exact experience of the first ever audience, then the answer is yes, it is hopeless. And if that experience gets more and more diluted the further away we get from the original show, then we're in a sorry state indeed. There is a level on which we'll never be able to recapture the 'true' music that the Greeks enjoyed or respond to it in the way the original audience did. But in a sense, that's true of almost all history. We weren't there when the American Declaration of Independence was signed, or when Britain's Glorious Revolution was staged. We can't know what it was like to be there – not fully.

But we do retain records left behind from those times – some were left intentionally, like political documents and historical accounts, while others simply happen to have survived thanks to the accidents of history, like the ruins of ancient Greek theatres and shards of ancient pots. Already in this book we've reviewed documents that tell us where Greek music was performed and looked at visual representations which seek to record those performances in one way or another. In the chapters to come we'll read descriptions of what it felt like to listen to Greek music – what emotions it elicited, and what sort of speculations people made about its place in the universe.

If there's no consistent human nature – no common thread that links us to all people, past, present, and future – then we have no reason to expect that these ancient documents would make sense or convey to us real aspects of musical experience. But if that's true, then there's really no such thing as valid history at all. In order to study anything that happened before our own lifetimes, we have to believe that human experience remains at least partially intelligible and communicable across generations. It's important to keep reminding ourselves how much has been lost, so we don't fool ourselves into thinking we know everything. But we needn't despair entirely: there is a lot that has survived.

This chapter has been about the places and times in which fifth-century Athenians performed their music, and it has argued that each performance had a link to its original venue which is in some sense unrecoverable. But we have also seen that by imagining our way into those venues, and observing how their specifications and customs would have affected composers, we can do a lot to picture Greek musical culture in a more vivid and detailed way.

We can never go back to the Theatre of Dionysus. As the sixth-century BC Greek philosopher Heraclitus famously observed, you can't step in the same river twice: the stream is constantly flowing onwards and being replenished with new water. Still, though, we can go back to the remains of the theatre, test what's left of its acoustics, and read the plays that were written to be performed there. We can read what people wrote about the music that accompanied those plays, and we can even catch snatches of that music written on a few precious papyri. We can't interpret any of that music perfectly – even if we did have the full score of an Athenian tragedy, we would bring our own preconceptions and modern assumptions to it. But we can make an approximation, and that's not nothing. The river flows on, but even so, all is not lost.

Some further reading

To learn more about the structure of a Greek theatre, it may be useful to refer to a book titled *The Architecture of the Ancient Greek Theatre*, edited by Rune Frederiksen, Elizabeth R. Gebhard, and Alexander Sokolicek (Aarhus: Aarhus University Press, 2015).

David Raeburn, a translator of Greek and Roman poetry, has written a book called *Greek Tragedies as Plays for Performance* (Oxford: Blackwell, 2016) which does a good job of thinking about some important stagecraft concerns for putting on Greek plays in their original settings.

Oliver Taplin has done much the same thing as Raeburn but with a closer focus on stagecraft, especially in his careful study, *The Stagecraft of Aeschylus* (Oxford: Oxford University Press, 1977).

Naomi Weiss is a scholar who has written a fair amount recently about the musical elements of tragedy and their cultural significance. In 2017, she published a book called *The Music of Tragedy* (Berkeley, CA: University of California Press), and in 2019 had a chapter titled 'Generic Hybridity in Athenian Tragedy' published in the book *Genre in Archaic and Classical Greek Poetry* (edited by Margaret Foster, Leslie Kurke, and Naomi Weiss, Oxford: Brill, pp. 167–190). Both can be useful for thinking through the original performance contexts of tragic music.

On the subject of comedic music, musical developments in the fifth century BC, and musical parody, Andrew Barker's essay 'Transforming the Nightingale' is well worth reading (in *Music and the Muses*, edited by Penelope Murray and Peter Wilson, Oxford: Oxford University Press, 2004, pp. 185–204).

For more on the distinction between occasional and architectural spaces for Greek music, see Sylvain Perrot's chapter in the forthcoming *Blackwell Companion to Ancient Greek and Roman Music*.

On the music of comedy in Rome, and its various settings, the definitive book is *Music in Roman Comedy* by Timothy J. Moore (Cambridge: Cambridge University Press, 2012).

On performance contexts for choral performance, one helpful recent chapter is 'Genre, Occasion, and Choral Mimesis Revisited, with Special Reference to the "Newest Sappho", by Gregory Nagy (in *Genre in Archaic and Classical Greek Poetry*, edited by Margaret Foster, Leslie Kurke, and Naomi Weiss, Leiden: Brill, 2019, pp. 31–54).

Since vase painting and other visual art is one of our main sources of information about both venues and instruments in ancient Greece, it's well worth taking a look at *Music and Image in Classical Greece* by Sheramy Bundrick (Cambridge: Cambridge University Press, 2005).

4

Education

*'Then the schoolmaster taught his pupils a song . . . either
"Pallas, Great Sacker of Cities," or "The Shout Heard Round the
    World" –
Keeping the harmony tight which their fathers had handed down.
And if one of them messed around or riffed some fancy riff,
The kind those fancy riffers learn from Phrynis nowadays,
He got beat good and sore for drowning out the Muses.'*

Aristophanes, *Clouds* 966–72

This is a speech from a comedy by Aristophanes, the raunchy parodist mentioned in the previous chapter. His concern in this play, *Clouds*, was with education – with the kind of teaching that young boys got when their parents sent them off to expensive schools. Speaking very generally, Aristophanes saw two very different forms of education on offer in Athens: the traditional style, in which tomorrow's best and brightest were schooled in the good old ways of doing things (and smacked on the behind if they tried to stray from those ways) and the dangerous newfangled approach, in which smart-alec whippersnappers were instructed in subtle arts of rhetoric and relativism.

As often with Aristophanes, this is a distorted caricature for comedic effect – there was surely a range of pedagogical philosophies in Greece beyond just these two extremes of traditionalist indoctrination and sophisticated radicalism. But the play does get at something fundamental about how wealthy young males were regarded, and what was at stake in their education. Since young men grew up to lead Athens – into or out of war, towards or away from new policies and practices – it mattered tremendously how they were taught to regard the received wisdom of their forefathers.

Music, including the poetic words which constituted its lyrics, was a central part of that. Would the young accept the age-old rules that their teachers endorsed, learning by rote the recitation of Homer and sticking to the old ways of singing the standards? Or would they become seduced by the new styles being invented all around them, drawn like the rest of the listening public to the flashy experiments of daring kitharodes and auletes? And what about the rest of Athens, the people without access to ritzy schools where they would be drilled in the classics? What kind of music would they learn, and how?

So in fact, this one passage – from a speech by a character called 'The Righteous Argument,' who represents traditional values – tells us a lot about the range of possibilities for musical education in Athens. There's a vision in it – albeit a silly and partially imaginary vision – of a traditional education, one with an accepted canon of suitable songs for learning. We don't have copies of the two tunes mentioned in this speech, respectively entitled *Pallas Persepolis Deina* or 'Pallas, Great Sacker of Cities' and *Tēleporon Ti Boama* or 'The Shout Heard Round the World.' But whether real or fictional, they are clearly meant to stand in for time-honoured classics – well-known songs that the students' 'fathers traditionally sang' – each of them kept meticulously free of modulation or melodic experimentation.

Old standards and new styles

This solemn and elevated form of traditional education was a load-bearing pillar at the centre of elite Greek society. Many Greeks, Plato among them, were fond of saying that there are two halves to a complete education: gymnastics for the body, and music for the soul.[1] This is where it becomes important to remember that 'music' and 'gymnastics' aren't the narrow modern concepts that those English words usually describe. These are the Greek words *mousikē* – the study of arts over which the *Mousai*, Muses, took precedence – and *gymnastikē* – physical activities which were traditionally done *gymnos*, in the nude (among them things like acrobatics, wrestling, and discus-throwing).

The Muses' purview of *mousikē* included all intellectual and artistic pursuits: history, singing, mathematics, and even philosophy. Not all of those pursuits were what we would now call musical: not even the Greeks would have sung the prose histories of people like Herodotus or Thucydides. But we've seen already that many things – things like poetry and drama – *were* kinds of music for Athenians. And we'll see in the next couple of chapters that even Greek maths, philosophy, and politics were musical in nature too. And even the broad division between physical and musical education advocated by Plato wasn't strictly maintained in actual practice: Athenaeus, for example, tells us about a form of dance called the *gymnopaidikē* (a word meaning something close to 'physical education') in which boys would rehearse stylized versions of wrestling moves.[2] Singing and dancing were crucial building blocks of classical Greek education because they represented the distilled version of something that, in one way or another, underlay almost all the humanistic and cultural practices that Athenian society held dear.

So boys learned music. Especially they learned to recite chunks of epic verse by Hesiod and Homer – these were the repositories of religion, allegory, and legend that educated men would cite regularly whenever they wanted to appeal to ancient wisdom. Epic, and especially the *Iliad* and *Odyssey*, were the closest thing to a bible that the Athenians (and the Greeks more generally) had. There was no central scripture for Greek religion that we know of, but Homer often served many of the same purposes as scripture: he was cited as the great recorder of worthwhile beliefs, stories, and observations about the world and its divine overseers. Schoolboys were taught to memorize and recite Homer so that they could enter productively into a society that used his epics as a main point of reference for cultural discussions.

They were also taught more advanced music, both vocal and instrumental. Here, again, it was considered of the highest importance that elite boys be cultivated in just the right way. The Greek word *nomos*, which refers to an individual song for recitation or performance, also means 'law' – learning the right way to do music, then, was the first step towards learning the right way to do politics. Opinions differed on just how much instruction of this kind was proper, but most schools certainly included some basic scales on a simple lyre and a little bit of singing. As detailed in Chapter 2, not all instruments were regarded as suitable for cultured gentlemen. Too much expertize in music of any kind, moreover, was regarded as beneath the gentry by the most conservative critics. Hence Aristotle recommended that boys, though they should study music for the refinement of their characters and sensibilities, should nevertheless stop short of technical virtuosity and paid performance. And heaven absolutely forfend that they should think of learning to play the *aulos*![3]

As always, of course, these proclamations may be more marginal and utopian than their authors would have liked us to believe – Plutarch, in his biography of the controversial gentleman and politician Alcibiades, does note that he refused to play the pipes.[4] But in doing so, Alcibiades had to resist the encouragements of his own teachers – so it's likely that the *aulos* actually was more accepted as a subject of high-class training than Aristotle would have liked it to be. That there was a generally accepted canon of learning, however, and that certain songs and styles were more palatable to traditionalists than others, seems beyond doubt.

Such was the philosophy undergirding decorous elite education of the kind envisioned in *Clouds*. At the same time, in that same passage with which we began, Aristophanes lets us in with a wink on a big open secret: the kids aren't really grooving to the golden oldies they have to learn in school. Instead, the more irrepressible among them have been known to wander into adventurous territory, mimicking the trendier artists popular among the younger set. Phrynis of Mytilene was one of the edgy kitharodes who came into his own during the days of the late fifth century BC, and he features in the *Clouds* quote above. 'New Musicians' like Phrynis (a term they never applied to themselves, but which modern scholars have invented to describe the trends of the late 400s) used to test out complicated modulations and melodic contortions.

So Aristophanes opens the door onto a more informal and tacit form of music education. It has always been the case – and still is today – that impatient young musicians who grow bored with formalized classical training will turn to their favourite artists for *ad hoc* training in the kind of things they really want to play. Guitar teachers lament that their pupils ditch Bach for John Mayer, or rigorous classical training on the organ falls by the wayside as kids rush to the electric keyboard. Even artists who do train classically sometimes leave the older ways behind in a bid for more pop relevance – this was the move that both Regina Spektor and Lady Gaga made to launch their careers in the early 2000s, for example. In Athens, even as schoolteachers handed down the classical learning of the old days, Athenian boys learned to test out hotter licks by imitating what they saw and heard onstage.

And, as a matter of fact, it was elite boys who performed in some of the most popular choral songs and dances of the Athenian year – notably, the dithyrambic and tragic contests at the City Dionysia featured young citizen boys selected in groups by the chorus-leader and trained specifically for the year's performance.[5] In those performances, boys would have been exposed to music like that of Euripides, which was known for its transgressive innovation. As a result – even if the sterner moralists disapproved – upper-class boys probably did get both training in and exposure to newer, more innovative forms of music.

Meanwhile for less well-heeled boys, or girls who didn't get a classical training, informal learning by emulation may have been the primary or the only way to get good at music. Plato laments at several points in his dialogues that attendance at the theatre and at concerts actually came to *supersede* the old ways of education as a means for the public to learn its morals and its tastes.[6] Certainly musicians themselves were keen to learn from one another and even steal one another's secrets. Timotheus, in his song *Persians* (lines 202–37), looks back on a succession of past innovators who went before him, whose compositions he studied and whose style he used as a model for his own (before surpassing them completely of course, at least in his own estimation). 'In the beginning Orpheus ... produced the dappled tortoise-shell lyre,' sings Timotheus,

'and after him came Terpander ... who yoked his Muse to ten chords.'
It's a stylized, semi-mythological reference to the invention of new
instruments and instrumental modifications described in Chapter 3:
building off of Orpheus' simple tortoise-shell, Terpander experimented
with new notes and modulations so that Timotheus could build on his
work by adding yet more.

The important point in all this for us isn't that Timotheus really did
learn directly from Terpander specifically, or from Orpheus (who may
never really even have existed). It's that he clearly saw himself as the
next in a long line of sound musical practitioners, each looking back to
the others' trailblazing work and building on it in his turn. This is a kind
of music-learning based on apprenticeship and rivalry – formal and
informal relationships between expert musicians in which one player
teaches another, or two contemporaries sharpen one another's skills
through professional competition.

Some of the artistic exchanges that arose in this climate were
legendary in every sense of the word: they both produced amazing
work and were probably exaggerated in memory beyond all proportion.
There are claims in the biographical tradition of Euripides that he
collaborated with Timotheus and that the two even composed a few
songs together. Even if that's not true, there are similarities in diction
and rhythm between Euripides and Timotheus which make it nearly
certain that the former learned a fair amount from watching and
listening to the latter. The great Lasus of Hermione is said to have
schooled Pindar, whose lyrical victory hymns were famous around the
Mediterranean. Formal schooling was one thing, but for professional
musicians and those outside the upper classes, informal emulation and
collaboration was just as important if not more so for music learning.

The *partheneion*

We do also get glimpses, although they're only glimpses, of a formal
music education that wasn't only for boys. Actually, one of the clearest

such glimpses comes not from fifth-century Athens but from Archaic Sparta. There, at least, people practised one important musical ritual associated with girls coming of age: the performance of a *partheneion* (plural *partheneia*). The word means 'maiden-song' or 'virgin-song': it very likely describes a communal dance to encourage and celebrate a young woman's entry into maturity and adult society.

The notion that Greek boys and girls should dance together in ways uniquely indicative of their gender and station in life – the practice of musical expression and celebration of what it means to be on the cusp of womanhood or manhood – is at least as old as Greek musical poetry itself.[7] But scholars have been particularly interested in the idea that certain girls' choral songs represent more formalized rites of passage. Think of the *quinceañera* celebrated by Mexican and Latin American communities when a girl turns fifteen: a large, ceremonial party for the gathering of friends and family to mark a transition into adulthood. Like *quinceañeras*, *partheneia* were very possibly a regular civic, religious, and social institution.

But unlike *quinceañeras*, *partheneia* would have been undertaken in groups – it wasn't just one guest of honour who presented herself, but a whole chorus of girls that did so together. In that respect, think more of a graduation ceremony, in which a whole class performs one communal ritual of self-presentation and group values. At the same time, a *partheneion* involved the participants learning and showcasing culturally important material, in this case a song and dance in the style of high Greek art. There are similarities there to the Jewish *bar* and *bat mitzvah*, in which young men and women recite a portion of scripture and give a talk to demonstrate their ownership and understanding of their traditions.

Imagining different aspects of those various festivals rolled into one gives something like the impression of what a *partheneion* festival might have been: part *quinceañera* celebration, part graduation ceremony, and part *bat mitzvah* ritual. There's some indication that similar rituals were practised in Sparta for boys, and girls probably sang and danced in choruses at various other times – not just as part of one big rite of passage. Probably the performance of *partheneia* was folded into a larger festival including various songs, dances, and rituals in celebration of a goddess (there has been much speculation about which goddess that might have been). But what's most interesting here is the girls' *partheneion* itself – both because it gives us rare insight into how young women were taught, and because we have extant examples.

Some words from a few *partheneia* have still survived until the modern day. One of the most revealing is the 'Louvre Partheneion' composed by Alcman, a lyricist from the seventh century BC. The fact that the words to these songs were written by well-known musicians like Alcman (Pindar also wrote some) tells us something off the bat: *partheneion* performances weren't exercizes in writing and composition, but demonstrations of learning and assimilation into the traditions of mainstream society. Girls didn't write their own music for these displays, nor did their teachers write music for them. Instead, pupils showed that they were entering woman's estate by memorizing and perfecting a work by a recognized cultural authority. As with boys' elite education in Athens, formal education for girls in Sparta seems to have had less to do with creativity than with tradition and cultural unity.

And Alcman's words themselves make reference to a hazy figure who may tell us a little more about what musical life was like for Spartan girls. Hagesichora (a name which means 'leader of the chorus') appears as the *khoregos* (a word which also means 'leader of the chorus'). Every Greek chorus had a *khoregos* – the tragedies which appeared at the City Dionysia, for example, featured a chorus with a leader as well. So did the dithyrambs written by masters like Bacchylides, Lasus, and Pindar.

Usually, the chorus leader not only took the lead in performance, but also helped to teach the chorus members. In this case, when those members are young girls learning to become adults, it's reasonable to assume that Hagesichora was their mentor and leader. Perhaps the name is a way of making Alcman's composition distributable among various different schools and groups of girls, so that they would have something to call their teacher regardless of her actual name. In any case, the lyrics are passionately admiring of her: 'the flowing hair of my

kinswoman Hagesichora blooms on her head like imperishable gold'
(lines 45–54).

The word 'kinswoman' is probably more affectionate than literal
here – it's not certain, and indeed it's quite unlikely, that all girls in a
chorus were related to their leader by blood. But this leadership figure
was obviously meant to be regarded with a kind of reverence that went
beyond respect for her purely musical skills. She is represented in the
song as a model of beauty and grace, a figure for the girls to admire and
probably emulate. In the lives of these girls, then, music wouldn't just
have been an academic subject to be theoretically analysed and
memorized by rote. It was a ritual that taught decorum, a cooperative
endeavour that would enable the girls to keep their poise in polite
society and school them in the shared literature of their parents and
grandparents. By dancing and singing the *partheneion*, young girls both
demonstrated and developed their social awareness.

All of this needs to be qualified somewhat with a warning that has
become somewhat ubiquitous in this book: there's lots that we don't
know. That bears repeating here because we've ventured outside of
Athens and, as mentioned in the introduction, one of the major reasons
for studying Athens is that it left behind a wealth of written records
when compared to other city-states. When we start talking about
Archaic Sparta, the picture gets still hazier. Nevertheless, it's important
to survey what we can, because it lets us broaden our picture a little bit
to the rest of Greece outside of Athens.

Unreliable narrators: the case of Spartan music

Alcman's *partheneion* is a rare treasure because it comes from an
actual Spartan. Many of the other things we think we know about
Spartans (like the stories about how they cut strings off of Timotheus'
lyre in Chapter 2) come from later authors with Athenian sympathies –
that story about the strings, for example, comes from a famous first-
century-AD essayist named Plutarch. Plutarch eventually became a

Roman citizen, but he read the great books and treatizes which were mostly written in Athens or by people who had studied there. As a result he, like many other authors who have left behind stories about Sparta, was writing from a distinctly Athenian angle – you might say he was more interested in using Sparta as a foil for Athens than in finding out the real truth about Spartan life.

That said, Plutarch and people like him are in many cases all we have to go by, and chances are good that they didn't just make things up out of whole cloth. What's more likely is that, here as always, we need to take what we read with a grain of salt – remaining aware that ancient authors, just like modern ones, can be biased.

For example: Plutarch also leaves behind what he claims is a record from the work of the Archaic-era Spartan legal reformer, Lycurgus. Lycurgus changed Sparta's laws to make them more democratic, much as Solon and Cleisthenes did in Athens. Among Lycurgus' reforms were careful instruction for the education of the youth, because Spartans no less than Athenians were concerned to make sure that children grew up to be good and productive citizens as a part of a healthy regime.

It seems music was a part of this: young girls, Plutarch says, were instructed to dance and sing at certain festivals. This passage is rich with colourful details about Spartan pedagogical practices, including a note that boys and girls both would perform in the nude to encourage fitness and self-confidence.[8] But what Plutarch says also contradicts to some extent what Aristotle has to say about music education in Sparta, which is that young nobles were trained in music theory and appreciation, but that they disdained the notion of actually performing themselves.[9] Given Plutarch's claims about bold public singing and dancing on the part of Spartan youth, and given that we have copies of *partheneia* which show us that young women did sing and dance at regular festivals, it's quite possible that what Aristotle says isn't strictly true.

It may be that Aristotle's account reflects a more restrictive attitude that developed after the time of Lycurgus, during the fourth century in which Aristotle himself wrote. But it may also be that

Aristotle exaggerated the reality of Spartan strictures. This is a good example of one case in which it pays to read our reports sceptically, holding one up against the other to keep them honest.

Aristotle, after all, talked about Sparta in Book 8 of his *Politics* because he wanted a contrast with Athens. He was considering whether young children ought to be trained in some level of musical performance – not too much, so they became vulgar, but just enough so they could know their way around a lyre. Perhaps music education in Sparta was somewhat limited and restricted – perhaps girls learned to dance in *partheneia* but weren't encouraged to learn a wider variety of songs and dances. Aristotle, on the other hand, wanted to advocate a decent variety of music as part of public education – he even wanted to go farther than his teacher, Plato, and say that people should learn some songs just for fun and relaxation, as well as edification.

In order to make his point, then, Aristotle may well have exaggerated by saying that the Spartans don't teach their children to perform *at all*. In that case, what he likely observed was that the Spartans were careful and restrictive in what they did teach their children, and he blew that out of proportion so he could establish a contrast between Athens and Sparta. Notice that this leaves us with some analytical work to do, but that it's not entirely hopeless: as usual, our record is imperfect but, with careful sleuthing, it can yield a basic picture of how life in and around ancient Athens worked. If Sparta was careful about what kinds of songs were taught to children, and if Athenians like Plato wanted to be similarly careful about musical education, then maybe Aristotle simplified things in order to advocate for a more liberal Athenian approach in contrast to the Spartan restrictions.

Putting it together

The more detailed we get, the more guesswork we have to do. But we can pull back the camera now and focus on some basic points we've learned from Plutarch, Plato, Aristotle, Aristophanes, and Alcman, all together. For one thing, both Sparta and Athens used music as part of their training for young people as they reached maturity, a fundamental tool for helping children to become adults and operate well in polite society. For another thing, there was always a range of opinions about just how much music children ought to learn, and for what purposes.

For some, like Plato and perhaps Lycurgus, music education ought to be limited to just those kinds of songs and dances that could be considered useful and instructive for budding citizens. In one of his more restrictive moods, Plato suggested that children – and indeed all good Greeks – should be restricted only to learning hymns and choral songs which describe and affirm the laws of the city.[10] Others, such as Aristotle, wanted to include a few more pleasurable tunes just to let the kids have a little fun and relax as a way of getting rejuvenated for further study. These differences of opinion bear witness to an ongoing conversation among the Athenian and Spartan upper crust about the best way to incorporate music in a course of study for upstanding young people.

It remains a constant, however, that Greek education not only included music but was saturated with it. This is something that remains true today about music education: it's not just about learning music. Sometimes a music class's primary function is to teach a particular song, instrument, or style, as when a student goes to a private instructor for singing, say, or guitar. And it does seem, for example, that schoolboys in Athens routinely had dedicated instruction in singing and playing the lyre. But just as often, music serves a purpose within a wider, integrated educational whole: we use songs in modern schools to memorize mathematical equations ('x equals negative b, plus or minus radical . . .'), or to express institutional pride (as in a school song), or to foster group cohesion (as in a football anthem). In this sense, the Greek concept of *mousikē* turns out not to be so foreign after all: there's more that is musical in our society than just the dedicated performance of song and dance.

In fact, there is a much later Greek scholar – Pollux, who studied and worked in Athens during the second century AD – who tells us that the word 'chorus' was sometimes used in Greek to mean not 'a group of coordinated singers and dancers' but simply 'a school'.[11] *Choregos*, likewise, didn't only mean 'a leader of singers and dancers' but also simply 'a teacher'. This reflects a wider Greek tendency, not only to see the world as filled with *mousikē* of all kinds, but also to use melody and rhythm to express the order and logic that underlay all sorts of larger social structures. In the next few chapters we'll see how political science, ethical reasoning, and even the movements of the heavens seemed to many Greek thinkers like a kind of music all their own – since all of them involved an intricate harmony of disparate parts brought together like different notes in one scale or song. Education, too, not only included music but was fundamentally musical – it could be looked at as an orchestration of distinct individuals into one harmonious whole.

In the case of education, those individuals were the citizens, and the whole was the city-state. We have seen in this chapter how singing, dancing, and the teaching of both were crucial ways in which young Athenians and Spartans were introduced into the customs and traditions of their respective societies. We have also seen that any break in that chain of instruction – any deviation from the old standards or attempt on the part of young people to explore more daring forms of music – was regarded with the utmost seriousness by teachers and cultural authorities.

In between formal education, amateur experimentation, and professional apprenticeships, there evolved a delicate dance of continuity and innovation which made up the musical life of the city-state. Who learned what, and why, was more than just an artistic question – it was an issue which struck at the heart of Greek society. Athenians and Spartans alike viewed music, and the education in humanities of which it was a central part, as a core of civilized social life. What kids learned in school would determine what they sang at drinking parties, which plays they voted for in the theatre, and whether they funded or even pursued professional music. All the cultural values and evaluations associated with those choices – many of which we have been studying in the previous chapters – were formed and instilled during those crucial childhood years. In the next chapter we'll see just how important the Greeks thought those values could be, and how high the stakes of them were.

Some further reading

The idea that the *partheneion* can be understood as related to ritual initiations into womanhood is defended in Claude Calame's *Les choeurs de jeunes filles en Grèce Archaïque* (*Choruses of Young Women in Archaic Greece*), published by Edizioni Dell'ateneo & Bizzarri in 1977. For summary of and engagement with the various scholarly responses to that idea, a good place to start is 'Visual Imagery in Parthenaic Song' by Laura Swift (in *The Look of Lyric*, edited by Vanessa Cazzato and André Lardinois, Leiden: Brill, 2016, pp. 255–87). On the larger festival occasion and which goddess(es) may have been worshipped at it, see 'The Occasion and Purpose of Alcman's *Partheneion* (1 *PGMF*)' by Robert D. Luginbill, in *Quaderni Urbinati di Cultura Classica* (volume 92, number 2, 2009, pp. 27–54).

There has recently been some discussion about whether classical Athens – typically regarded as having been very restrictive when it comes to public choral performance by women – did in fact allow female choruses to perform in certain contexts. On this score, have a look at 'Another Look at Female Choruses in Classical Athens' by Felix Budelmann and Timothy Power, in *Classical Antiquity* (volume 34, number 2, 2015, pp. 252–95).

One excellent old book, *Ethos and Education in Greek Music* by W.B. Anderson (Cambridge, MA: Harvard University Press, 1966) remains among the go-to authorities on the relationship between music and education in Greek life. For more discussions of musical ethics in education, in addition to the references at the end of the next chapter, see 'The Good and its Relation to Music Education' by Yaroslav Senyshyn, in *Philosophy of Music Education Review* (volume 16, number 2, 2008, pp. 174–92).

For more recent discussions of how ancient Greek musical knowledge was passed down, see the following:

There is a lovely chapter on 'Musical Education in Greece and Rome' by Stefan Hagel and Tosca Lynch in Wiley Blackwell's *Companion to Ancient Education*, edited by W. Martin Bloomer (Hoboken, NJ: Blackwell, 2015, pp. 401–12).

On the selection of citizen boys for the dithyrambic and tragic choruses, see Helene Foley's 'Choral Identity in Greek Tragedy' in *Classical Philology* (volume 98, number 1, 2003, pp. 1–30).

See also 'Ps. Plutarch, "De Musica". A History of Oral Tradition of Ancient Greek Music' by Egert Pöhlmann, in *Quaderni Urbinati di Cultura Classica* (volume 99, number 3, 2011, pp. 11–30).

Politics

The ethics of music – *ēthos* and *mimēsis*

Here are three quotes from three very different people:

'Poets are the unacknowledged legislators of the world.'

'Politics is downstream from culture.'

'A city's musical fashions never change without a change in the most important laws as well.'

The first of these is a line from the 'Defence of Poetry' by Percy Bysshe Shelley – the poet, womanizer, and radical activist at the forefront of England's Romantic movement in the nineteenth century. The second is a favourite saying of Andrew Breitbart – the American political firebrand whose website, breitbart.com, became an incendiary platform for zealous supporters of Donald Trump after Breitbart's own early death. The final quote is attributed to Damon of Athens.[1] Damon was the controversial fifth-century BC musical theorist and intellectual whom many suspected of pulling the strings behind Pericles' rise to power over the Athenian people.

These three would have agreed on very little else, but they are all unanimous on this point: art shapes politics. The trends which direct public life are formalized in legislation, but they get their start in the theatre and the concert hall. That idea goes right back to ancient Athens, where music was understood to be a powerful force for cultural change. According to Damon and other influential Greek thinkers, it was music that had the power to shape the hearts and change the minds which would eventually conceive the city's laws. At first glance, it might seem like music theory is a long way off from political theory these days –

like Spotify and Carnegie Hall are a far cry from the mess and mudslinging of Congress and Parliament. But in the view of some ancient Greeks, harmonies and rhythms were powerful tools for shaping the moral character of young men, who would in time grow up to lead governments and pass legislation. For those who believed this, even a small change in musical fashions meant a seismic shift in the values and laws that governed civic life. Where did they get that idea?

The answer lies in the notion of *ēthos* – character. As far back as the eighth century BC, Greek poets and thinkers connected different kinds of music with different kinds of personality, emotion, or disposition. By the fifth century, in Classical Athens, this had become a kind of conventional wisdom: melodies and rhythms were thought to have an emotional flavour or feeling which made a song into more than just a pretty tune. One typical way of making this claim was to associate different keys or 'modes' (sequences of intervals which dictated the notes that could be played in a song – see Chapter 7) with different moods. The Dorian mode, for example, was supposed to sound manly, brave, and forceful: it was good for expressing military courage. The Mixolydian mode, by contrast, had a reputation for being dramatic and mournful: it suggested the most abject kinds of wailing and grief.

We have similar ideas about our own music nowadays. There's a kind of simplified popular notion that minor-key songs sound sad and major-key songs sound happy, and some songs do fit this pattern well. Beyoncé's 'Love on Top' is an example of a stereotypically 'major-key' number – bright, poppy chords, chipper lyrics, and an upbeat tempo. Meanwhile 'Summertime,' the melancholy jazz number that opens George Gershwin's tale of love and loss, *Porgy and Bess*, is in A minor.

But things aren't really so simple. Taps, the melancholy bugle call which memorializes soldiers slain in battle, only uses three notes – and they're three of the most important notes in the major, not the minor scale. Meanwhile, the Beatles' wistful 'Yesterday' is rooted in a major scale but incorporates lots of minor chords which help give the track its air of regretful nostalgia. Generalizations like 'minor is sad and major is happy' get at basic trends, but the reality in practice is much more complex. Songs can express many more moods than just 'happy' and 'sad', and the difference between those moods doesn't just boil down to different types of scale. Metre, tempo, interpretational choices in live performance – all these things and more give a song its emotional colour.

Something like this was true in Athens too: there was a huge array of rhythms, scales, and musical styles (see Chapters 7 and 8), and thoughtful musicians noticed that these differences made for different kinds of mood in each song. But that elaborate musical diversity could get oversimplified in layman's terms or even in philosophical theory. So Plato, in his *Republic*, suggests an invariable link between military courage and the Dorian mode: only Dorian can 'represent the pronunciation and intonation of someone being manful in military action' and facing down enemies with steely-eyed determination. He assigns similarly rigid roles to the other modes: Phrygian tunes mean steadfast temperance, but the Mixolydian equals tears and histrionics.

Other thinkers may not have been quite so strict about the rules. Aristoxenus (the music theorist whom we met in Chapter 1) seems to have been one of the people who believed that it was foolishness to assign one emotion to one mode in a simplistic way. Instead, Aristoxenus suggested that all of a song's features come together to create an emotional experience. There is a unique profile of tempo, rhythm, mode, melody, and so on that helps make each song what it is – these many stylistic and structural details make Handel's 'Hallelujah Chorus' feel different from, say, Kanye West's 'Heartless.' For those who followed Aristoxenus' thinking, a song's emotional coloration resulted from this complex blend of different musical features.[2]

What does any of this have to do with *ēthos* – with character? For many Classical Greek philosophers, a person's moral character was closely connected to the different kinds of emotions that person tended to feel. In fact, Aristotle argued that the word *ēthos* (with a long 'e') came from the word *ethos* (with a short 'e'), meaning 'habit'.[3] According to this line of reasoning, one's moral character is determined in part by how one habitually feels in various given situations.

So, for instance: if someone were sitting quietly at home with a coffee when suddenly an ogre broke down the door and demanded to duel to the death, he or she might react in a number of ways. Maybe this is the kind of person who would typically react to that situation by feeling terrified, which in turn would prompt him or her to run frantically away and hide behind the nearest throw pillow. That would mean this person had the vice of cowardice. But maybe another person could be counted on to react with confidence, feeling ready or even excited to face the ogre down. That person could be said to have the virtue of courage. When certain emotional responses get engrained in us and become habitual, they contribute to our virtues and vices – they become aspects of our moral character.

The point of all this for us is: according to people like Plato and Aristotle, music didn't just make its listeners feel a certain way. Over time, it conditioned those listeners to feel that way routinely, and so it helped shape their moral characters. To give a very basic example: if you were repeatedly exposed to lots of Dorian-mode songs with lyrics about winning glory in battle, then your soul would be trained to associate feelings of triumph and courage with ideas of battle and valour. The modern equivalent would be grooming soldiers by making them listen to rousing anthems like 'I Vow to Thee My Country' while they train. Then when the time came to charge into the fray, they'd instinctively get fired up with feelings of resolve that would prompt them to take on their enemies without flinching. That is, the music they listened to would have shaped their characters, which would make them more likely to act in the right kinds of ways. Roughly speaking, that's how music was usually linked with *ēthos* – songs produce emotions, which form moral habits, which stimulate ethical actions (the word *ēthos* is where we get our modern word, 'ethics').

Plato and Aristotle weren't the only ones who believed these things. For example, one second-century-BC Stoic philosopher, Diogenes of Babylon, wrote a book *On Music* in which he adopted Plato's view almost exactly.[4] There are popular anecdotes preserved by all sorts of authors which tell how masters like Damon and Pythagoras used certain kinds of songs to develop students' virtue, or to calm rowdy lads out on the town whose parties had gotten out of hand.[5] These are probably just tall tales, but there's a kernel of truth in them: musicians and musicologists in Classical Athens thought their craft had great power to direct young people's development towards emotional and ethical maturity. In fact, this opinion was accepted widely enough that we only have one early objection to it, preserved on a papyrus from the third century BC. The author of this 'Hibeh Papyrus' had to dig in his heels against a number of self-styled musical experts who 'say that some songs make people self-disciplined, others prudent, others just, others brave, and others cowardly.'[6] It's clear that this was a belief with more than a little currency: the kind of music you listen to helps shape the kind of person you become.

Ancient Greek scholars offered a lot of different explanations why music had this kind of power. I already gave a hint about one such explanation, one which very quickly gained lots of traction. When I quoted Plato's assertion that the Dorian mode can 'represent the pronunciation and intonation' of a particular kind of speaker, I was translating a notoriously untranslatable Greek word: *mimēsis*. In its most basic and broad sense, *mimēsis* means any kind of mimicry or reproduction (it's where we get words like 'mime'). This noun (and the related verb, *mimeisthai*) was used to describe children playing make-believe and adults imitating foreign accents.[7] In Aristophanes' comedy, *Frogs*, the goofy weakling Dionysus dresses like the brawny champion Heracles in the hopes that some of the hero's derring-do (and social clout) will rub off on him. Dionysus tells Heracles that this getup is *kata sēn mimēsin*: that is, 'in imitation of your style.' Dress-up, imitation, play-acting – these ideas have obvious connections to what artists do when they try to represent the world around them in paintings or on the stage. So *mimēsis* quickly became associated with the artistic act of 'representation' or even 'depiction.'

Plato used *mimēsis* in all these ways, and he was especially concerned with dramatic *mimēsis* at the theatre and in concerts. He had a lot of different and sometimes quite opaque worries about the kind of *mimēsis* that artists perform. For one thing, in Book 10 of the *Republic*, he seems concerned that arts like painting are deceptive because they present flimsy copies of the things we see around us in the world, which are themselves only pale shadows of an ultimate, ideal reality beyond our own. But those more abstract ideas won't really come into play until the next chapter, when we think about music and the galaxy. For now we can focus on another, more pedestrian kind of artistic *mimēsis*: the expressive imitation involved in onstage performance.

Here's something screamingly obvious: when an actor acts, he pretends to be somebody else. If I play the part of Oedipus the King, I'm trying to move in particular ways and speak with particular inflections that make my audience understand what kind of person Oedipus is: in a certain sense, I want you to see and hear Oedipus, not me. I have noted already that much of theatre in fifth-century Athens was musical, and that much of the most popular music was performed onstage. Tragic and comic performances, kitharodic solos, recitations of Homer: these all came with their own rhythms and melodies or sing-song intonations. And all of them involved 'playing a part' or 'putting on a character' to some extent. In the *Iliad* Book 1, for example, Homer tells the story of Apollo's old priest, Chryses, who implores the Greeks to give back his beloved daughter. Plato says that when Homer – or anyone reciting Homer – delivers Chryses' speech, the artist behaves 'as if he had become Chryses.'[8] That's even more true for actors: an Athenian man onstage would have used every tool at his disposal to transform into Oedipus, or Dionysus, or Orestes – from his mask and his costume to the motions of his hands and the sound of his voice.

Especially the sound of his voice. Even today, the human voice is one of the most powerful tools for artistic expression. In a massive ancient theatre with top-notch acoustics, audiences would have listened to hear the story and the characters brought to life in speech and song. The way the actors used their voices would have helped to express how their characters were feeling, and what sort of people they must be to feel that way.

Here is another, less obvious fact: Ancient Greek has what's called a pitch-accent. This is a set of markings over particular syllables which dictate where the pitch of the voice has to travel, even when you're speaking without music. Everyone who reads Greek has seen these accents plenty of times, but not everyone knows what they're there for. The acute accent (´) tells the speaker to go up in pitch. The circumflex (˜) means a rise up followed by a fall back down, and the grave (`) means that, even though this syllable usually has an acute accent, it doesn't in this case and the speaker shouldn't raise his or her pitch. So with higher sounds written in boldface, lower ones in plain type, and vowels which slide from low to high and back again written in bold capital letters, here is a basic approximation of how one might read aloud Antigone's line from Sophocles' play, 'behold me, oh citizens of my fatherland,' or, ὁρᾶτ' ἔμ', ὦ γᾶς πατρίας πολῖται: *horAt' **em' O** gAs patrias pol**I**tai* (line 806).

What this means is that even regular everyday Greek speech had a kind of melodic quality to it. In fact, the first-century-BC literary critic Dionysius of Halicarnassus called this movement the 'melody of spoken language' – the predictable motions of the speaking voice up and down in pitch.[9] The more traditional musicians tried to match the melodic contours of their songs to these 'natural' contours of spoken pitch, so that the tunes their characters sang made a kind of heightened representation of the way they would speak in real life. An actor in a play or a character in a sung narrative wouldn't only say the kind of words that character would say – he could actually sing them on the kind of melody that the character would use in speech.

And so, for traditionalists, melody and rhythm were an important part of the *mimēsis* that actors and songwriters make in their art. If I'm a brave soldier facing down an enemy, I'm going to choose different words, with different pitch-accents, than if I'm a coward getting ready to head for the hills (thus I might exclaim, 'bring it on, ogre!' rather than, 'I say, it appears I've soiled myself'). Artists who depict those different kinds of characters, then, can use melodies to communicate those feelings and the movements in pitch that they generate.

There's more. Recall that moral characteristics like cowardice were connected in Greek theory to emotional experiences like fear. Those emotional experiences were themselves connected to pleasure and pain: a theorist of this kind might have said that brave people, for example, take pleasure in honourable victory and feel pain at the very idea of ignominious defeat. And those pleasures and pains actually push their souls in specific directions. Plato, in the *Laws*, uses the image of a puppet being pulled by strings: the pleasure that good citizen-soldiers feel pulls them in the direction of valour, leading them on into battle at the appropriate moment rather than pushing them away into retreat.[10] Which means that moral qualities are made out of movements, just like the melody of speech is made out of movements. As the soul moves towards triumph and away from shame, the words one speaks and the songs one sings move up and down the scale to imitate those soul-motions – to make a *mimēsis* of them. Think of Henry the Fifth in Shakespeare's play, desperately outnumbered but rousing his men to the charge: 'once more unto the breach, dear friends, once more' (*Henry V* Act 3, Scene 1, line 1). On the Greek stage, those words could have been sung with a stirring Dorian melody that captured the pull Henry feels towards the glory of one final valiant charge, and the push he's giving his troops to follow him.

Again, the reality was more complicated. For one thing, innovative composers often broke the pitch-accent rule, using their melodies to express unexpected emotions or surprize the audience by moving in different ways than normal speech would. And, of course, actors could do much more than just move up and down the scale: they could sing louder or softer, or emphasize certain words, using the full array of musical variety to express the full range of emotions. All of those details could go into producing a nuanced musical performance expressing powerful and complicated feelings.

Many of these ideas have roots deep in Greek history and thought, not just among scholars like Plato or Aristotle but also among poets and musicians themselves. Ancient Greeks as far back as Homer drew links between personal character and musical habits: in Book 3 of the *Iliad*,

Homer has the Trojan hero Hector scold his brother Paris for being overly interested in playing his lyre – as if that had softened his manly resolve and left him unsuited for war.[11] Aeschylus, who wrote our earliest surviving Greek tragedies, says that the sound of trumpets in battle stimulated such courage that it 'set fire' to the hearts of those who heard it.[12] We've seen already how certain kinds of music were assigned to men and others to women, and there were those in Athens who felt that Damon's own musical research was part of a sinister secret plot to sway the hearts and minds of powerful Athenian politicians like Pericles.[13] In theory and in practice, in and out of Athens, in the fifth century and beyond, music in ancient Greece was much more than just noise: the songs you listened to, and the way you listened to them, swayed your emotions and so became part of your identity and your role in society.

Music in society

By now we're starting to see why Damon might have thought music was so important for politics. 'A city's musical fashions never change without a change in the most important laws as well': if melodies and rhythms mould young souls, and young souls grow up to be state leaders, and state leaders get to write laws, then a society's musical tastes are the seeds of its legal and political systems. The moral character of the elite boys whose musical education we studied in Chapter 4 was therefore crucially significant. It would have mattered intensely to parents and teachers that such boys be raized with the right tunes in their ears.

That's why Plato won't allow the youngsters who will eventually lead his perfect Republic to listen to anything other than the Dorian and Phrygian modes. It's why Aristotle's comments about musical education come at the end of his book on *Politics*, which itself is the sequel to his book on the moral formation of young men, the *Nicomachean Ethics*. Looking back on the history of Rome, Aristides Quintilianus wrote that 'when the body politic had experience with leaders who lacked musical acculturation, she witnessed the reality of what Plato prophesied in the *Republic* – she saw her citizens ruthlessly shedding one another's blood.[14] The musical training of a city's impressionable leaders-to-be was literally a matter of life and death for anyone who would live under the laws written by those same young people.

This wasn't just an abstract intellectual exercize for the Athenians. Think of all the parts of life in ancient Greece which had music at their centre. Consider again the slaves who entertained their masters at drinking parties, and the boastful songs the masters themselves would sing to show off their skills. The trumpet tunes that Greek generals would use to rouse soldiers into battle. The musical celebrations that were awarded to leaders and noblemen when they won athletic competitions, and the pride which Athenian leaders took in hosting musical contests of their own. Consider, too, that the songs we now think of as music were only supposed to be the audible version of a much bigger *mousikē* – an overarching social, moral, and cosmic order which governed the whole universe. Athenians in the ancient world heard songs almost everywhere they went, and those songs were more than just a background soundtrack. They were statements about how life ought to be lived, tools for teaching the public and reinforcing – or, in the wrong hands, undermining – the social order.

Maybe this seems silly. When Plato outlaws artists like Homer and the tragedians from his ideal state because their songs don't portray the right kind of morality, he often sounds to modern readers like a fussy old curmudgeon at best, and a kind of proto-fascist at worst. The notion of a society getting so worked up about art that they would condemn musicians to exile feels foreign, even primitive – imagine a piano teacher having to flee the country because she taught too much Brahms and not enough Bach.

But we go too far if we dismiss Greek concerns about musical morality as outdated and irrelevant to our own enlightened age. For one thing, the idea of keeping Homer and Euripides away from impressionable young minds only sounds absurd because ancient authors have an air of dignity and cultural cachet for modern readers – to us, these are paragons of high culture. Teachers and parents go to great lengths to encourage their protégés to read Greek epic, not to forbid it. But read just these three lines from the *Iliad*: 'the stone crushed both his temples, and the bone didn't hold firm – his eyeballs fell out on the ground in the dust at his feet.'[15] The poem is shot through with innumerable moments like this which describe and even relish the hideous violence of war in lurid detail. If we filmed these moments in a movie – if we really took them seriously not just as highbrow poetry but as graphic and powerfully affecting imagery – we probably wouldn't let young children watch them. Modern parents, just like Plato, tend to monitor the content their children take in, shielding them from more adult themes until they're ready.

In fact, parents today have still more in common with Plato and Damon. Plenty of sensible adults are concerned about the effects that musical rhythms and melodic patterns can have on growing minds. One need only google 'negative influence of heavy metal' or 'dangers of hip-hop' to find article after article wondering whether hardcore club music is bad for tender young listeners – not only because of misogyny and aggression in the lyrics, but because of the developmental effects of throbbing beats and repetitive melodies. In 1987, the University of Chicago Professor Allan Bloom published his explosive book, *The Closing of the American Mind*, in which he argues that university students are being corrupted by, among other things, the vicious sensuality laced through music by such beloved stars as Mick Jagger. Those students, wrote Bloom, 'know exactly why Plato takes music so seriously. They know it affects life very profoundly.'

Some of these modern concerns are more focused on content – on what is said in a song's lyrics – than on the rhythmic and melodic forms that so worried ancient theorists. But modern commentators worry about form too: in 2009, the American Academy of Pediatrics published an article entitled 'Impact of Music, Music Lyrics, and Music Videos on Children and Youth,' in which was cited a range of studies about the neurological and emotional influences exerted by certain kinds of rhythm and melody. The same set of debates was brought back into the public eye in 2018 when Kendrick Lamar became the first rapper to win the Pulitzer Prize for his album, *DAMN*. Central among the controversies which swirled around that award was the question whether Lamar's music could be considered morally suspect, and whether that made it unsuitable for a place of high cultural honour.

What this comes down to is: Greek fears about *ēthos* might sound old-fashioned at first, but we still have to reckon with similar anxieties about music and art. In fact, we use music as a social and political tool too: at athletic events, for example, we use songs to bind people together, to express and to engrain shared values, no less than Peisistratus did in Athens. Now just as then, musical culture is a high-stakes moral and political game. I began this chapter by quoting Damon alongside Percy Shelley and Andrew Breitbart – two much-maligned figures with very different views, but united with Damon in their conviction that, in Breitbart's words, 'politics is downstream of culture.'

Many people through the years have found these ideas challenging and troubling. Even those who want to take music seriously may still be vehemently opposed to limiting the free range of its expression. Those who disagree most strenuously with Plato feel that art can and should present not only the admirable parts of human life but also the dark and perverse corners of our experience – not just the triumphs that make us noble but the pain and anguish that make us human. Forbidding musicians to explore such emotions won't prevent the rest of us from feeling them – it will only repress our expression of them.

But for those who feel that way, it's important to wrestle with the full force of Plato's arguments – and with those of Damon and Shelley and Breitbart and Bloom. We can't write them off as fuddy-duddies or scoff at them as if we were past all that. To the contrary, a deeper understanding of the Greek ideas in this chapter is vital for anyone who wants to argue robustly against them. It remains an enduringly open question how parents should help their children to grow into morally responsible leaders and adults, and what role musical training should play in that process. But Homer and Aeschylus, Damon of Athens and Diogenes of Babylon – for all their flaws – remain important and worthwhile interlocutors in this ongoing debate. In many cases, the terms in which that debate is framed and the consequences which are associated with it go directly back to fifth-century Athens, and to the musical ideas we have been studying all throughout this book. Those ideas are not only historical relics or arbitrary abstractions – they are central sources for our own modern quest to live commendable lives and govern just nations. There are few more pressing reasons to study Greek music.

Some further reading

Mimēsis and *ēthos* are both fiendishly difficult concepts to understand. But for a more detailed study of the former word and its afterlife beyond Greece, it's hard to do better than Stephen Halliwell's book, *The Aesthetics of Mimesis* (Princeton, NJ: Princeton University Press, 2002). For the latter concept, one classic is Warren D. Anderson's *Ethos and Education in Greek Music* (Cambridge, MA: Harvard University Press, 1966).

The *Blackwell Companion to Greek and Roman Music* has sections on 'Conceptualising Music' and on 'Music and Society' with several entries relevant to this chapter: see especially Destrée's 'Musical Ethics', and Csapo and Wilson's 'Music and Politics in Greece'. For more advanced study, a classic is Csapo's 'Politics of the New Music' (in *Music and the Muses*, edited by P. Murray and P. Wilson, Oxford: Oxford University Press, 2004, pp. 207–48).

Those keen for more on Damon can review the very comprehensive gathering and analysis of sources published by Robert W. Wallace, *Reconstructing Damon* (Oxford: Oxford University Press, 2015). But a must-read to understand the changes Plato probably made to Damon's views is Tosca Lynch, 'A Sophist "in Disguise"' (*Etudes Platoniciennes* volume 10, 2013) – available online at https://journals.openedition.org/etudesplatoniciennes/378.

An engaging new book by Armand D'Angour, *Socrates in Love* (London: Bloomsbury, 2019) gives a perspicuous overview of Pericles' social and intellectual circle, Damon included (chapter 4, 'The Circle of Pericles').

Diogenes of Babylon's musical work is buried within the badly damaged prose of Philodemus' *De Musica*. The most recent edition is by Daniel Delattre (Paris: Les Belles Lettres, 2007). For a clarifying analysis of this difficult text, see Linda Woodward, 'Diogenes of Babylon Reading Plato on Music' (in *Aristotle & the Stoics Reading Plato*, edited by V. Harte, M.M. McCabe, R.W. Sharples, and A. Sheppard, London: Institute of Classical Studies, 2010, pp. 233–53.

To get better acquainted with the gorier bits of Homer, check out the endlessly amusing and impressively virtuosic infographic from *Greek Myth Comix*: http://greekmythcomix.com/comic/deaths-in-the-iliad-a-classics-infographic/.

The Cosmos

In Act V, Scene I of Shakespeare's *The Merchant of Venice*, the dashing lover Lorenzo sits his darling, Jessica, down on the ground. The night is silent, but Lorenzo says he hears music:

> How sweet the moonlight sleeps upon this bank!
> Here will we sit and let the sounds of music
> Creep in our ears: soft stillness and the night
> Become the touches of sweet harmony.
> Sit, Jessica. Look how the floor of heaven
> Is thick inlaid with patines of bright gold:
> There's not the smallest orb which thou behold'st
> But in his motion like an angel sings,
> Still quiring to the young-eyed cherubins;
> Such harmony is in immortal souls;
> But whilst this muddy vesture of decay
> Doth grossly close it in, we cannot hear it.

There's no audible music playing – only 'soft stillness.' But, says Lorenzo, an attentive observer can pick up on a silent kind of harmony that emanates from even the 'smallest orb,' from every planet in the sky as it moves along its orbit. Human beings, because they are made of flesh and blood (a 'muddy vesture of decay'), can't use their sluggish ears to hear this divine sort of music. It's beyond our form of hearing – we have to use our minds to intuit it.

In just twelve lines, Shakespeare has given a pretty decent summary of a central idea behind Greek musical philosophy. This idea is sometimes called the 'music of the spheres,' and Shakespeare could take it for granted because it survived long after ancient Athens was no more than a memory. The basic concept is that planetary movement and the structure of the universe are 'tuned' like a musical composition: the distances between planets are proportional to the distances between notes on a scale, and their movements follow the same patterns as the movements of air which generate melodic sound. In fact, for some ancient theorists, this inaudible cosmic motion was the more fundamental, the more truly *musical* kind of music. Our audible songs, generated by human hands and mouths, were just a pale fleshly echo in the material world of a deeper, more pure cosmic music.

Shakespeare can put all this in the mouth of a suave young lover because, in the sixteenth-century Renaissance culture of Elizabethan England, Classical ideas were gaining a great deal of traction. The notion that heaven is a harmony was so compelling that even many respectable physicists set out to prove that it was literally true. This may sound silly to us now, and so our question in this chapter will be: what on earth gave the Greeks this idea? Why did it seem plausible to people like Plato and the Pythagoreans that human music was a reflection of some grand universal design? And what was it about that belief that stuck?

Numbers in the sky: Pythagoreanism and mathematical cosmology

We should start with Pythagoras. Or at least, we should start with the Pythagoreans. Pythagoras himself, like Socrates, never wrote anything down in his efforts to contemplate the secrets of the cosmos. But based on the reports of his followers and the ideas which came to be associated with him, it seems fairly plausible that he believed numbers are, in some capacity, the building blocks of the universe.

At the very least, many of Pythagoras' followers spent a great deal of time trying to work out the basic mathematics that undergird the shape and structure of the material world. Philolaus, who was a famous member of the Pythagorean school in the fifth century BC, claimed that all things in the universe are known through numerical understanding.[1]

For Pythagorean theorists like Philolaus, numbers weren't just basic tools for counting things in the world like oranges and horses. They were concepts that made the whole universe possible.

This is less outlandish than it may initially sound. Even today, when physicists study how the universe works, they almost always do so by trying to calculate the movement of planets and molecules in a way that makes mathematical sense. Newton's second law of motion (force equals mass times acceleration, or $f = ma$), Einstein's theory of relativity (energy equals mass times the speed of light squared, or $E = mc^2$), and the various elaborate theories that make up the ever-evolving science of quantum physics, are all attempts to describe the world using numbers. That's because what we usually think of as numbers – the standard figures like 1 and 2 – are really stand-ins for much deeper patterns and concepts which describe fundamental truths about the universe. 1 doesn't equal 2, because one thing can only be itself, not something else: if these sorts of things sound basic in the extreme, that's because they are. They're the essential realities which mathematics describes and which make the world what it is.

There is a famous story – apocryphal, but still telling – that Pythagoras recognized the mathematical relationship between harmonious notes when he heard anvils being pounded in a blacksmith's shop. By the end of the fifth century, Pythagoreanism had become associated with the idea that musical notes and the relationship between them were just audible versions of those foundational mathematical truths that also govern the rest of the physical universe. As a result, some Pythagoreans – such as Hippasus (early fifth century), Philolaus (*c.* 470–*c.* 385), and Archytas of Tarentum (active in the first half of the fourth century) – became interested in discovering the exact ratios which produced various harmonies in the musical scale. Some of these philosophers – most notably Archytas – demonstrated an interest in the actual practices of real musicians. But for the most part, Pythagoreans weren't running the numbers because they wanted to get the tuning on their *kitharai* just right – they weren't known, in other words, for their stellar concert performances. What they were interested in was music as a sensory way of accessing deeper truths that undergirded the whole universe.

Compare this with Aristoxenus, who, though he began his career as a Pythagorean, eventually rejected the mathematical vision of music in favour of a more intuitive, empirical approach. Aristoxenus' treatizes on music theory are hugely important for understanding the Greek scale today because they are devoted to music *as it is* – the notes and harmonies that actual musicians really used. Or at least, the ones they *should* have used according to Aristoxenus – he still had his own very definite ideas, after all, about the right way to tune a lyre. But those ideas were definitively based on what Aristoxenus thought worked in practice – on the experience of a listener appreciating or disliking a particular set of intervals. If the ideal interval sounded good, but didn't correspond exactly to a neat mathematical ratio, so be it: Aristoxenus was not one to let maths get in the way of beauty. A somewhat enigmatic group of earlier theorists whom Aristoxenus calls 'harmonicists' (*harmonikoi*) were also known for their empirical interest in musical harmony and rhythm as actually heard 'in the wild' at live performances.[2]

Not so the stricter Pythagoreans. For them, beauty *was* maths: they believed that everyday melodies should conform to the purest abstract mathematics that theorists can use to describe it. That's because the mathematics, not the music, came first and foremost as a basic feature of reality. This could be put another way by saying that what we think of as music – the audible sounds of notes and harmonies – was only one small part, and not even a very important part, of the broad science of *mousikē* that interested the mathematical mystics of the Pythagorean tradition. That science included tunes and songs, but it also included numbers and equations, which in the last analysis were more central as a way of understanding the world.

This Pythagorean version of mathematical music made it easy to draw links between songs and the stars. Because if what we hear when we hear music is a pale human reflection of the most basic mathematical relationships, then intervals like the fifth sound beautiful to us precisely *because* they are arranged according to principles that govern the rest of the material world as well. Planets in their orbits, according to this theory, move in ways that are governed by the same basic principles as govern the rules of harmony. It would be only natural, then, that really well-tuned music would conform to the structure of the heavens, because both are patterned after one set of pure mathematical truths.

A short history of the entire universe: Pythagoreanism according to Plato

This vision of the universe actually made its way into the work of Plato, who wasn't a Pythagorean but who apparently took a profound interest in the mathematical and musical researches of Pythagoras' followers (especially Archytas, who once sent a ship to rescue Plato when he was being detained for political reasons by the king of Syracuse). One of Plato's dialogues, the *Timaeus*, contains an origin-myth that tells the story of the whole world in Pythagorean terms. It's worth summarizing that myth briefly, because it can afford some insight into how the Pythagorean tradition could be used to build one big coherent theory of music, maths, and cosmological physics.

The *Timaeus* is presented as a sequel to the *Republic*, Plato's massive dialogue in which Socrates and his friends try to draw up a blueprint for the perfect political organization. Supposedly taking place on the day after that massive conversation unfolds, the *Timaeus* features a speech by the title character on the nature and origins of the universe. To hear Timaeus tell it, the whole cosmos was created by a single god. That god – he was called the 'demiurge,' which is a Greek word for 'craftsman' – made the universe as a single, perfect, living organism. From the model of that vast, living cosmos, all other living beings were created in imitation.

This massive, animate universe was constructed perfectly by the demiurge in the shape of a sphere, with planetary orbits rotating within one another at determined intervals. The distances between those intervals were picked by the demiurge very precisely, according to specific ratios. And so according to Timaeus, the whole universe is fashioned with reference to the same mathematical proportions as a musical scale (the Dorian scale, to be precise). In fact, the correspondence between musical and planetary intervals is no accident. The notes of a well-tuned scale sound good to us because we instinctively recognize within them the same mathematical ratios that dictate the perfect structure of the universe.

This elaborate myth is a way of giving narrative shape to the Pythagorean traditions of musical cosmology that were developing in Plato's day. Timaeus' story is an artistic way of representing two major ideas which were current by then: that the whole cosmos is structured according to mathematical principles, and that music could be analysed in terms of the ratios underlying various harmonies. If maths governs the universe, and music is just audible maths, then music must be governed by the same deep numerical truths that guided the construction of the cosmos itself.

It turns out that this pair of ideas helps support the political and ethical theories of music from Chapter 5. Because Timaeus goes on to explain that all human souls are little carbon copies of the universal soul in miniature – our own inner lives are like pocket-sized versions of the heavens. And the movements of our souls – those impulses towards and away from things which are the rudiments of our desires and emotions – are finely calibrated according to the same set of ratios that order the solar system, the universe, and the notes of a well-tuned scale.[3]

That's if all goes well. If our souls and our desires are perfectly ordered, Timaeus says, then we'll act reasonably and want all the right sorts of things. Everybody will live in harmony just like instruments in a perfectly unified orchestra, playing along with the vast and precise music of truth that governs the universe.

This, of course, is not what happens. The world in which we actually live is fraught with wars, cheating, petty theft, and all manner of human misbehaviour. If the universe is music, it sometimes seems horribly out of tune. This, according to Timaeus, is a problem that arises from the fact that our souls have to operate within physical bodies. The process of embodiment was a disorienting affair, and the result of it was that we don't always act the way we should. Sometimes our desires get away from us and we hurt one another out of greed, lust, or pure spite. These kinds of disorderly desires and feelings come to us because our soul's divine motion has been thrown out of whack by the fleshly vicissitudes of our earthly body.

That's where music comes in. Music helps us to realign the motions of our soul with those of the cosmos, because according to Timaeus, it 'has movements akin to the revolutions of the soul within us.' Good, well-tuned music can re-calibrate our psychological movements. So, for example, a bracing song in the Dorian mode could spark the courage in the heart of a soldier who has gotten tired and just wants to run home to bed. The proper musical motions would bump his soul back into the proper psychological motion, towards glory and away from shame.

The Unified Field Theory of everything

There are some scholars today who think that the whole ethical tradition of music comes from this set of Pythagorean ideas. Certainly there were lots of legends about Pythagoras using music to calm down rowdy drunks when their souls and desires got out of hand. Damon, the rhythmic ethicist whom we met in the last chapter, seems like he may have collaborated a bit with an aulete named Pythoclides, who some people think might have been inspired by Pythagoras. But this is to reach far back into the shadows of speculation, probably further back than can realistically be trusted. What seems clear is that these two major strands of Greek thought about music – the cosmic music of the spheres and the ethical music of the soul – formed two halves of what would eventually become one giant 'Unified Field Theory' of musical mysticism: a Greek-inspired vision of the world and everyone in it as governed by a mathematical, musical logic.

That 'Unified Field Theory', though, was still developing and changing long after Pythagoras, Damon, Plato, Archytas, and the rest were all long dead. The philosophers we've been following so far really just laid the groundwork for the beginning of something much bigger than themselves – a way of thinking about music that would far outlast their own lifetimes.

In the ancient world, the direct inheritors of musical cosmology were the Romans. One high-profile representative of Roman musical cosmology was Cicero, the polymathic and often insufferable genius whose hardnosed statesmanship helped shape the era just before the Roman republic ended. Cicero had a lot of side-hobbies outside of politics, and philosophy was chief among them. Plato and the Stoics both interested him immensely, and both of them believed in the ethical, cosmological powers of music. Cicero wrote his own *Republic*, only fragments of which are still extant. In one of those fragments, a main character (the republican war hero Scipio Africanus) says that the best kind of sound is

> that which, using tones separated by unequal but nevertheless carefully proportional intervals, is caused by the rapid motion of the spheres themselves … Learned men imitating this harmony on strings and with their singing have earned their way back to this region [of the heavenly spheres], as have those who have cultivated their talent at searching for divine truths.[4]

We can hear Timaeus echoing in the background there, and we can also hear the rumblings of what will become Shakespeare's poetry: 'such harmony is in immortal souls.'

Elite Roman intellectuals didn't just bring musical cosmology to Rome. They also eventually, as their empire expanded, exported Greek ideas about music to a vast portion of the known world. Boethius, who lived during the fifth and sixth centuries AD just after the deposition of the last Roman emperor, wrote down what he saw as the core principles of Greek musical philosophy in a book called *On the Fundamentals of Music*. Right at the outset, this book presents a vision of three interlocking planes of reality, all of them governed by the same musical and mathematical rules. There's the cosmos, with its planets moving along their orbits – these emit a kind of harmonized sound too profound for the human ear to hear. Then there's the musical union between a human body and soul, which if properly tuned keeps both together in a peaceful and righteous whole. And finally there's the kind of audible music we make with instruments and on the stage.

These three types of music – human, planetary, and instrumental – are linked together by one set of mathematical ratios for Boethius just as they are for Timaeus. In fact, Boethius quotes Timaeus in his opening chapter. *On the Fundamentals of Music* was one of the primary vehicles for preserving and popularizing Pythagorean and Platonic musical philosophy in the centuries after Rome fell. It was so influential that for generations after him, medieval schools taught a curriculum called the *quadrivium*, inspired in part by Boethius' description of the Greek arts. *Quadrivium* means 'four paths' or 'four studies,' and it refers to the four ways of studying mathematics in the Pythagorean tradition: arithmetic, geometry, astronomy, and music.

Proclus, who lived in the fifth century AD shortly before Boethius, wrote that music was the branch of mathematics which taught 'the relationship between quantities.' In other words, the discipline of music was about measuring and understanding the proper way to bring disparate elements into order. In a sense, that summarizes perfectly all the different kinds of *mousikē* that have emerged over the course of this book. Cosmic music is what makes the planets move in a well-orchestrated pattern, at a perfect distance from one another. Human music is what makes the relationship between a soul and a body work, teaching the soul how to manage its pleasures and emotion in the right proportion and moderation. And when we sing and dance, we use movements and tones to form a picture of these deeper, more sophisticated sorts of music – audible songs are structured in a kind of artistic imitation of the profound logic that binds the whole universe, and our own inner lives, together.

Planetary sheet music

This vision of a cosmos hung perfectly together in delicate, musical balance was tremendously compelling in the medieval period as a way of looking at the world and our place in it. It remained so compelling, for such a long time, that many scientists whom we still regard highly today thought the music of the spheres was a perfectly valid astronomical idea. In the late 1500s and early 1600s, the German visionary Johannes Kepler set out to map the motions of the heavens and understand their logic more perfectly than had yet been done. He was so successful that his three major observations, the three 'laws of planetary motion,' are alive and well today as important rules of cosmological physics.

The third of these laws describes a mathematical relationship between a planet's distance from the sun and the length of its orbit. That relationship is articulated at the very end of a book Kepler wrote called *Harmonices Mundi* – the Harmonics of the World. The whole of this book is dedicated to proving the basic idea of planetary music: Kepler wanted to show that there are basic relationships inherent in the structure of our solar system which conform to the basic relationships that govern musical scales.[5] Even his use of the word 'harmonics' is a kind of use that would only be possible for someone inspired by Greek philosophy: Kepler meant to describe not just audible harmony but the foundational resonances and tensional relationships that give rise to the pleasant sounds we hear in everyday music. The *Harmonics of the World* is a majestic sketch of the universe as a choir of planets, kept in balance and harmony by the mathematical rules that govern their relationships. The third law of planetary motion is the fruit of Kepler's work in that area, and it is therefore a piece of scientific knowledge that we still owe, in some sense, to the Greeks and their music of the spheres.

And it's possible we owe more than just that. When we began this chapter, much of its contents may have seemed ridiculous. Certainly it is possible that many modern readers will find it difficult to believe in a demiurge or anything like one – the idea of an actual architect shaping the world with his own two hands may come across as a little primitive at first. But then, a literally physical demiurge of the kind you may have begun by imagining – a flesh-and-blood creator god of the kind one could see and touch with one's own two hands – would have seemed like a primitive idea to Plato too. Or to most of the Greek intellectuals who thought seriously about music and philosophy. In another one of his dialogues, the *Phaedrus*, Plato has Socrates say this about the task of describing something eternal and spiritual: 'to describe it just as it is would be a work of immense and divine explication. But to say what it is *like* would be a smaller task, fit for a human being.'[6]

Socrates was talking in the *Phaedrus* about the 'Form' of the soul, the essential reality of what it truly is. But it's safe to say that his comments apply to any case in which a Platonic dialogue tries to say what things are like *beneath the surface* – what the essential realities that underlie the material world are like. Mathematics is one such reality: it's a set of intangible ideas that undergirds the entire tangible, visible, physical universe. Maths is something you can't see or touch, but it's threaded through the whole structure of space-time in a profound way.

The real nature of these deep truths is something beyond the human mind's capacity to grasp. Einstein said once that 'behind anything that can be experienced there is a something that our mind cannot grasp and whose beauty and sublimity reaches us only indirectly and as a feeble reflection.' Almost by definition, we can't directly perceive the ideas underlying the universe, because we're *part* of the universe. It's like a fish trying to see the water. That's why Plato used myths like the one in the *Timaeus*: they are intuitive, human ways of getting at truths behind and beyond all human perception.

Among those truths are the mathematical rules that govern the composition of the universe. And it is not so crazy to believe that these rules also govern the patterns that we hear and delight in when we listen to music. In some sense, this must be true, since music is a part of the physical world just like anything else. We still observe, all these years after Pythagoras, that the tones which sound harmonious to us are generated by vibrations in the air whose wavelengths are mathematically related to one another in predictable ways. Modern scientific studies show how these musical wavelengths, when properly tuned, resonate with emotional centres in our brains that direct our feelings and actions on a deep, pre-conscious level. Even unconscious people, as was discovered in a 2015 study in Lyon, France, can have brain activity stimulated and improved by music. And another study from Harvard University recently found that even people who do not understand the language of a given song can often intuit the subject matter and emotional intent just by grasping the song's musical structure.

At the very beginning of this book, I wrote that music is a human constant. To be sure, there are all sorts of variant patterns in the way we create music across the world and across time: the ancient Greeks themselves found some intervals harmonious that we would consider extremely strange, if not downright ugly. But anthropologists do observe that some things stay the same across cultures – things like a regular, rhythmic beat and a sense of melodic contour can be found pretty much everywhere humans live.

The point of all this is to say that, though the details of musical mathematics have evolved quite a bit since the days of Pythagoras, many of the basic ideas and observations stick with us, albeit in unrecognisable form. Music *does* appeal to the human mind on a deep emotional level, one which taps into the fundamental mathematical principles that govern our entire universe. It's no more crazy now than it was in the fifth century BC to say that music is an audible version of those principles, that it makes perceptible to our ears a set of truths that is otherwize imperceptible but nevertheless ubiquitous.

That's why philosophers, mathematicians, and poets alike are still captivated by the power of music, which exerts a force on our psyche that seems almost impossible to understand. Why, after all, should a set of notes played one after the other, or together in a harmonious orchestra, bring listeners to heights of joy and elation, depths of fear and anguish? Yet they do, still: from electronica to metallica to classical cantatas to R&B, every form of music that has ever been beloved got popular because it *spoke* to its fans on some deep, visceral level – because it tapped into the deepest workings of their hearts and minds and made them feel things in a way they couldn't quite explain. Whether one is more inclined to attribute that effect to brain chemistry, or divine providence, or some combination of both at once, it's actually quite difficult to articulate what music does without making some sort of reference to how it mobilizes the same forces that govern our hearts and direct the planets in their courses.

'Without music in its best sense there is chaos,' said the great twentieth-century Russian composer Igor Stravinsky in a 1948 article for the journal *Musical Digest*. 'For my part, music is a force which gives reason to things, a force which creates organization, which attunes things. Music probably attended the creation of the universe.' A Pythagorean would say, well, yes: in some sense, the creation of the universe *was* music, of the deepest kind there is. Greek philosophy contains some of the first and most profound attempts to describe music and its power while doing justice to all the different ways in which mathematics and melody seem to be intertwined. We are still in the debt of the Pythagoreans today, and not just because they showed us how to measure the sides of triangles: though our language and our science has developed and advanced, we have not stopped hearing the music of the spheres.

Some further reading

There are a few sources on Pythagoras and his relationship to musical numbers and ethics in the 'further reading' section of the previous chapter. For a little more on the modern science behind musical understanding across different cultures, start with Kathleen Higgins's book, *The Music Between Us* (Chicago, IL: University of Chicago Press, 2012).

Carl A. Huffman is justly famous for his searching accounts of Pythagorean thought. His books on Philolaus (*Philolaus of Croton*, Cambridge: Cambridge University Press, 1993), Archytas (*Archytas of Tarentum*, Cambridge: Cambridge University Press, 2005), and Pythagoreanism in general (*A History of Pythagoreanism*, Cambridge: Cambridge University Press, 2014) have much to recommend them.

Also on Pythagoreanism, for a highly modern and sceptical approach, see Leonid Zhmud's *Pythagoras and the Early Pythagoreans* (Oxford: Oxford University Press, 2012).

A few of the scientific studies which chart neurological reactions to musical stimuli can be found online. The study which showed reactions to music in unconscious patients (based in Lyon, France) – 'Boosting Cognition with Music in Patients with Disorders of Consciousness', *Neurorehabilitation and Neural Repair* (volume 29, number 8, pp. 734–42) – can be found at PubMed (https://www.ncbi.nlm.nih.gov/pubmed/25650390).

The Harvard study got a few write-ups in more popular journals, and so a good place to start reading about it would be in the *Harvard Gazette* (26 January 2018): https://news.harvard.edu/gazette/story/2018/01/music-may-transcend-cultural-boundaries-to-become-universally-human/.

The Albert Einstein quote is from his book, *The World As I See It* (*Mein Weltbild* in the German edition of 1934, but translated into English the next year). It is available in a 2014 edition by CreateSpace Independent Publishing.

Tunes

How scales work

This book has described and discussed a form of music most people have never heard. The development, culture, and philosophy of ancient Greek song is rich enough that much can be said about it even in the absence of first-hand experience. And indeed most people assume that no melodies can possibly have survived from so long ago. But in fact the ancient Greeks did have a system of music notation – a way of writing down the notes in a tune. There are sixty-one 'documents' – scraps of papyrus, inscriptions on stone, and in some cases manuscripts – which preserve written music from between as early the fifth century BC and the third century AD.

These are some of the most exciting things that survive from antiquity, and also some of the hardest to understand. It was in 1581 AD that the first known modern editions of Greek musical documents were published by Vincenzo Galilei (father of the famous astronomer). Ever since then, scholars have been trying to wrap their heads around the written music that comes down to us from ancient Greece. In the twentieth and twenty-first centuries, a burst of new research and discoveries helped experts to read Greek notation more accurately than ever before, meaning that with some careful effort we can now try – albeit without certainty – to hear snatches of music echoing across the centuries from the ancient world.

There's a tremendous appeal in such a prospect, of course, but since the research is still quite new it can be very obscure and technical. These final two chapters, therefore, represent an effort to distil some of the basics that underlie Greek melodic and rhythmic notation in a way that doesn't require a lifetime of study to understand. As such there is a world of detail left out here, but in outline and as a rough picture this will serve as an introduction to how Greek music was written down.

First, a little bit on how the Greek scale works. A 'scale' is a set of musical notes between two pitches that are an octave apart. Sing the first two notes of '**some-where** over the rainbow': 'some' is an octave lower than 'where.' In the Americas and Europe, most songs will use a set of eight notes that can be written within the span of an octave. In addition to the two notes of 'some' and 'where,' there are six others in between, and together they make up a scale.

The distance between two notes is called an 'interval' – an octave is one type of interval, and another very important one is called the 'fourth.' A fourth is smaller than an octave, meaning that its top note is less high in pitch above its bottom note. So, now sing the first two notes of '**here comes** the bride': 'here' is a fourth lower than 'comes.' There's just one other, smaller interval that needs mentioning for now, and that's the 'whole step' (or 'major second' or 'whole tone'). It's the gap between '**happy**' and '**birthday**' in the song 'Happy Birthday.'

Here's the next step: if you sing two fourths separated by a whole step, you get an octave. Try it:

1. Sing '**here comes** the bride,' then
2. Start on the same note as **comes** to sing '**happy birth**' from 'Happy Birthday,' then
3. Start on the same note as '**birth**' and sing '**here comes** the bride' again.

The last note you sing on **comes** in (3) will be an octave higher than the first note you sang on **here** in (1). Sing those two notes next to each other, and you'll find they're the same two notes as you would sing if you sang '**some-where** over the rainbow.'

Those two fourths are likely the skeleton of every scale most Westerners have ever heard, even if they don't realize it. There are two basic kinds of scale in modern Western music, and they are called 'major' and 'minor' scales. Even those who have never studied music may know the major scale: often people sing through it using the syllables 'do-re-mi-fa-sol-la-ti-do.'

The notes on the first 'do' and 'fa' are one fourth, and then from 'so' to the second 'do' are another fourth, just like the two **'here comes** the bride's in (1) and (3) above. Those notes stay exactly the same when we switch from the major to the minor scale, too: only the notes on 'mi,' 'la,' and 'ti' change.

It's important to remember here that one can begin a major and a minor scale on any note of the piano keyboard – or more precisely, on any 'absolute' pitch. The basic structure – the intervals between the notes that make up a major or minor scale – can be repeated starting from any note or pitch. So, a C major scale is what results when a musician starts on the note 'C' and then plays the eight major notes up to the next C an octave above, whereas an A minor scale starts on 'A' and then goes up to the next A, hitting the minor notes along the way. The word we use for the set of notes obtained by starting a scale on a particular note is a 'key': we say that a certain song is in the 'key of G minor' or the 'key of C major' depending on which notes it tends to use and gravitate towards. But no matter where the scale starts, and no matter whether it is major or minor, it will always have those two fourths separated by a whole step as its basis.

In its fundamentals, the ancient Greek scale worked in the very same way – in fact, one of the reasons our scales work the way they do is because Greek scales did so. The skeleton of any Greek scale may be outlined by starting on a given note and then going up a fourth.[1] After that, the scale would *either* go up a whole step and another forth to make an octave, as in a modern Western scale, *or* leave out the whole step and just stack a second fourth directly on top of the first one. Skipping the whole step creates a 'conjunct' scale (because the two fourths are conjoined together), whereas the modern Western scale is called a 'disjunct' scale (because the two fourths are disjointed by a whole step). One of the earliest forms of modulation (transfer from one key to another) was to keep the lowest notes of the scale the same up to

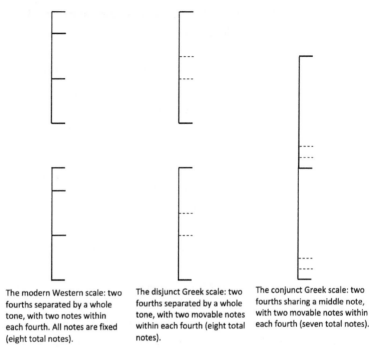

The modern Western scale: two fourths separated by a whole tone, with two notes within each fourth. All notes are fixed (eight total notes).

The disjunct Greek scale: two fourths separated by a whole tone, with two movable notes within each fourth (eight total notes).

The conjunct Greek scale: two fourths sharing a middle note, with two movable notes within each fourth (seven total notes).

Fig. 4 Diagram of disjunct and conjunct Greek scales compared to the modern Western scale. Spencer A. Klavan.

the central one, *mesē*, and then re-tune the higher notes to switch back and forth between the conjunct and disjunct forms of the same scale. The diagram on this page gives a bare-bones illustration of how this works.

Things get still more complicated. Much of the music produced today only uses two types of scale: the major and the minor. The Greeks had at least three basic types: the diatonic, the chromatic, and the enharmonic. This seems strange to modern listeners. We are used to thinking in terms of the piano keyboard, which divides the whole octave up into twelve 'half steps' (or 'semitones' or 'minor seconds'). This is the smallest available interval in modern Western music – the melody of the famous theme in the movie *Jaws* is simply two notes a semitone apart. But now try this: start by singing any note of your choosing, then slide all the way up to the note an octave above, without stopping. It's a continuous slide, which means there are actually an infinite number of pitches between every note. We happen to stop at the half step, but we could just as easily keep dividing that into smaller intervals and sing a third or a quarter step.

Those smaller intervals aren't playable on a keyboard – they would be 'in between' the white and black keys. But anyone with training and practice can sing them just fine. Greek musicians and audiences were used to them, which means quarter tones, though they sound unusual and out-of-tune to us, sounded quite acceptable to them. So starting with the standard two fourths, a Greek musician could then fill out the scale by putting different notes in between the fourths. If there was a quarter tone between each of the bottom, second, and third notes, that created what was typically called an *enharmonic* scale. A semitone between each of those same notes produced a *chromatic* scale, and one semitone between the first two notes followed by a whole tone between the second and third made another type of scale called the *diatonic* (when the first two intervals of the tetrachord collectively took up less than half of the whole tetrachord – as in the standard enharmonic and chromatic species – they were called a *puknon*, or 'bunch'). In reality, there were many more 'shades' (*chrōmata* in Greek) than just these three species – musicians could subtly adjust their strings or finger their pipes in any number of ways. But in ancient Greek music as in modern Western music, those two fourths always stayed the same – they were rooted in place and then filled in with notes that could change depending on the type of scale.

The series of four notes (the two fixed notes of the fourth and the two moveable ones within them) that served as the basis for a scale was called a 'tetrachord' (*systēma* in Greek), and a particular type of tetrachord (diatonic, enharmonic, or chromatic) was called a 'species' (*genos*). Just like our major and minor, these enharmonic, chromatic, and diatonic tetrachord species could be played starting at any pitch.

How we got here

This basic series of harmonic practices (and others besides) gave rise to a huge diversity of musical forms and traditions. Over time, efforts were made to form a unifying theory of how those traditions fit together, principally by fixing the various scales into a coherent system of shared pitches and relating them to one another.

The simplified and smoothed-out version of things presented here was probably not widely accepted until at least the very end of the Classical period. Musicians in the ancient world, after all, didn't have international conferences or universally standard textbooks. They met together to compete at different festivals around Greece, or collaborated in gatherings or guilds where they could share ideas and pass down traditional practices. That meant that different communities had different ways of doing things, and pockets of local custom would develop from place to place.

Much of the information I've been summarizing so far comes mostly from the work of Aristoxenus of Tarentum. Aristoxenus left behind a very complex treatise, made more complex because not all of it survives. The *Elements of Harmony* was meant to explain the principles behind all the different ways of writing and playing Greek melody – a kind of unified field theory explaining how all Greek scales worked. His system was quite successful and ended up being influential as musicians after him tried to standardize the way they played and wrote. But Aristoxenus was drawing together some of the major strands of thought that had gained traction before him, as well as rejecting some of the variations that didn't fit into his theory.

Terpander, another early musician called Olympus, and Pythagoras were all important predecessors to Aristoxenus who laid the groundwork for Greek music theory. It's not totally clear what each of them really invented themselves, and what their followers invented but then attributed to them. Terpander and Olympus were said to have tuned the strings on their lyres in a few simple ways which caught on and became the norm for professional musicians.[2] If Terpander and Olympus fixated on a few 'tunings' for their lyres, it means they deliberately chose to use a particular set of scales – a few sets of seven notes, each probably spanning an octave (for disjunct scales) or the slightly smaller interval of a 'seventh' (for conjunct scales). What these stories suggest is that, by the sixth century BC, musicians had a set of scales they liked to use and that might even have been standard for competitions.

It's worth noting that these early scales would have been fixed within the range of pitches that a lyre or an aulos can play. So instead of a series of modes in higher and lower pitch, there would have been a series of different note arrangements, all within the same pitch range but tuned differently. The most basic and common of these were called Dorian, Phrygian, and Lydian. But there were many others, and already by the fifth century (likely before), musicians were devoting themselves to finding ways of relating one pitch to another so as to modulate between them. Eventually theorists attempted to come up with a definitive model for these relationships using the 'Greater Perfect System' (the *systēma teleion meizon*). This was a standard sequence of intervals, originally developed to standardize the construction of *auloi* but – it turned out – useful much more generally as a tool for understanding the relationships between scales.

The Greater Perfect System spanned two octaves in *relative*, not *absolute* pitch (it could be mapped, that is, onto any series of pitches no matter how high or low). There was a bottom note (the *proslambanomenos*), followed by four tetrachords of which the first was conjunct with the second and the third was conjunct with the fourth. But the second and third were disjunct, separated by a whole tone, meaning that the centre of the system was a full disjunct scale spanning an octave. The tetrachords within this Greater Perfect System could be diatonic, chromatic, or enharmonic, depending on the species under discussion (see the diagram for further clarification).

Aristoxenus would argue that every important key could be obtained by starting on a different absolute pitch and progressing upward according to the sequence dictated by the Greater Perfect System.

Technically, the sequence dictated by the System could start on any note. But it was most useful for modulation if a central scale was fixed in place as a standard to which users could refer. This centre of the system (whose core was a disjunct scale with the *mesē* fixed at about the pitch of our modern b natural above middle c) came eventually to be called Lydian. But if the musician wanted to shift to a lower key he could treat the note below the *mesē* of Lydian (the *lichanos mesōn* of the Lydian) as the *mesē* of a new key, called Phrygian. One note below that came the Dorian –

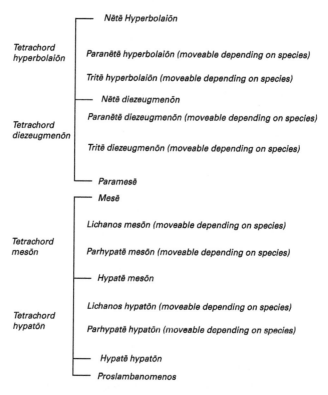

Basic diagram of the Greater Perfect System, with Greek scale degree names (cf. Chapter 2). Each note is named after its place within the scale (e.g. *lichanos, mesē*, etc.) and the tetrachord of the overall system in which it is placed (e.g. *hypatōn, dezeugmenōn*, etc.). Adapted from the diagram on page 13 of Andrew Barker's *Greek Musical Writings, vol. 2* (Cambridge: Cambridge University Press, 1989).

Fig. 5 Diagram of the Greater Perfect System with Greek scale degree names.

each of these proceeded according to the interval sequence of the Greater Perfect System, transposed up and down the absolute pitch spectrum.

As will have become clear, Aristoxenus applied names like 'Dorian' and 'Lydian' to fixed keys (*tonoi* in Greek) whose pitches were set within the Greater Perfect System. But those names had previously referred in many cases to particular tunings (perhaps originating from the particular regional or ethnic groups whose names they bore) which were not pitch-fixed keys at all but modes (*harmoniai*): sequences of intervals that could be played starting on any pitch. That local colour and variation was lost in Aristoxenus' system and the ones which followed it. But a major advantage of keeping all the keys mapped out onto one grid based on the Greater Perfect System was the ability to modulate (relatively) easily from one key to the next.

The motley crew: musicians, theorists, and everything in between at Athens

As Athens came into its own, it became a place where theoretical experimenters and practical performers alike tested new ways of developing and combining the ideas of older authorities like Pythagoras and Terpander. By the fifth century BC, musical scholars all over Greece were talking about Pythagorean theory and debating its finer points of detail. Some felt that numbers were the fundamental building blocks of the universe, and that Pythagoras' ratios were at the heart of music's beauty and power. Others thought that mathematical abstractions were too removed to capture the realities of live performance – they preferred to improvize based on their own feel for the music and go with what sounded good. Starting from traditional scales like the ones credited to Terpander, they played around with new ways of shifting between different keys in the middle of the song.

Others of a more Pythagorean bent were inclined to theorize and abstract music down to its essentials. Eventually these more mathematically inclined thinkers became known for experimenting with something called a 'monochord,' a simplified instrument with just one string that could be stopped at different lengths to produce different notes. With these and other techniques, they stripped the scale to its bare bones and attempted to describe its basic structure without reference to the messiness of live performance.

Some of the leading lights in Athens combined theory and philosophy with practical craftsmanship and performance experience. Lasus of Hermione was one of the earliest ones to do so: he was a music director and a composer in his own right, but also a writer and a theorist. Damon of Athens was another popular authority on music in the city – rich elites or up-and-comers who wanted the best for their sons would have sent them to the likes of Damon to receive the cutting edge of musical education. Celebrities like Damon and Lasus helped spur on the lively musical activity that continued throughout the fifth century.

That activity was particularly fervent in the second half of the 400s, as bold young artists made a series of changes to musical tradition and experimented with unorthodox styles. Timotheus of Miletus was said to have experimented with all sorts of new forms, ornamentations, and styles of modulation. Strict conservatives (like Plato) were against modulation and experimentation of this kind, because they threatened the purity of the more basic scales. These traditionalists accused performers like Timotheus of pandering to the public's taste for novelty at the expense of the more stately forms and traditions which had gone before – these were pretty tunes designed to titillate, but not to edify. That's probably pretty unfair, as Timotheus and his fellow innovators (people like Cinesias and Philoxenus of Cythera) were trained professionals who took meticulous care in constructing their melodies. They may have been radical, but they weren't careless.

And they were certainly crowd favourites. The written melodies which survive show that modulation did catch on, and Timotheus' songs, so shocking in their day, became old standards just a generation later. Think of rock stars like Elvis Presley and the Beatles, who appalled older listeners in their day, but who show up now on oldies stations as easy listening.[3] One artist who probably helped to popularize the new musical style in the fifth century was Euripides. Of the three great tragedians whose work survives from the fifth century, Euripides was the most experimental, prone to creative risks. He seems to have incorporated some of the trendier musical fashions from the concert stage into his own plays, and there are rumours that he collaborated professionally with Timotheus.[4]

As the fifth century unfolded, artists fed off of one another's energy with greater and greater enthusiasm, leading to an explosion in new tastes and forms. But they were still working from that basic harmonic structure – two fourths, each filled with two middle notes, to make a scale. Even as they went wild with ornamentation and experimentation, Greek musicians shared a few core theoretical elements with each other: no matter how new the music got, it was always rooted in that original scale structure.

Writing things down

It was because of this endless proliferation of new scalar forms and tunings that Aristoxenus did what he did. From the fixed set of early tunings that many early musicians used, Aristoxenus set out to develop a system in which one could transition easily from one key to another. That meant placing each tuning in a different pitch range and establishing the relationships between them, so that each one was distinctive, but related to the others, in the notes it used. That's the origin of the complicated system described above.

This also meant that Greek artists could share a system for writing music down. They may have had more than one such system, but only one survives, written out and explained in a handbook by the scholar Alypius of Alexandria in the fourth or perhaps fifth century AD. The notation itself is much, much older than Alypius – in fact, it almost certainly goes all the way back to the fifth century BC. So its creation might have been part of the flurry of discovery and creativity that we have been discussing in this book.

'Alypian' music notation (as it is now called by scholars) works quite differently from the graphic systems that we now use to write music down. In modern sheet music, the most widespread form of written notation uses something called a 'staff' – a stack of horizontal lines onto which composers write dots to represent notes. The dots are interchangeable in terms of pitch – an 'A' doesn't look any different in shape than a 'C'. But how high or low they are placed on the lines of the staff determines how high or low they ought to be played or sung.

In Alypian notation, there is no staff. Instead, the notes are written out on top of the song's words: each syllable has a symbol above it indicating the pitch that goes with that syllable. That means that every pitch has to have its own symbol. From the bottom of the lowest key to the top of the highest, every possible note in the scale is assigned a shape. There is one set of symbols for vocal music, and another for instrumentation – so a musician could tell by reading a piece of Alypian music whether he needed to sing the words on the notes indicated, or whether there needed to be accompaniment with a lyre or pipes.

The Alypian symbols basically correspond to the notes of the Greater Perfect System – that is, in their final form they were used to write music with the kind of orderly, coherent arrangement of keys that Aristoxenus put together. Aristoxenus was originally from the Pythagorean school, but he eventually studied under another philosopher, Aristotle, who emphasized experimentation and attention to real-life detail. So Aristoxenus made sure to devize a system that would describe as accurately as possible the real intervals and scales that sounded good to Greek audience members of his time.

But he also tried to find a theoretical scheme that would line up those scales in logical relationship to one another and create orderly routes to modulation in between them. That means he smoothed over some of the rough edges that come with live performance – the *ad hoc* techniques that expert performers devize in the moment. It's important to be aware of that so that we keep in mind how limited our knowledge is: as wonderful as it is to have written music from the ancient world, we have to remember that standardized systems for writing music are always a little bit artificial.

It's the same with music today: you can notate the melody of Taylor Swift's *Shake it Off*, but how can you capture on paper the little scoops and flips that her voice makes when she raps the bridge? Or how can you write out the way Bob Dylan's fingers grate against the strings of a guitar? The documents that survive give us a basic sense of some melodies which the ancient Greeks played and sang, and that's a huge gift. But there is a lot which we can only imagine or guess at from descriptions – things like the particular vocal quality of a performer, or the dynamics that musicians would have used to make their pieces exciting. What we're doing here is combining careful scholarly research with artistry and imagination to approximate something like what the Greeks might have heard.

An example will help show how it works. There is a scrap of papyrus in the Imperial Library of Vienna, Austria which was used as part of a mummy's wrapping in Egypt. Since papyrus was expensive, it was often recycled and repurposed to do things like wrap up corpses for burial. Some of the most precious writing from antiquity was discovered by accident because it was re-used as scrap paper. This particular papyrus is invaluable: written on it are a few lines from a play by Euripides called *Orestes*. The lines are from a song sung by the chorus after the title character, Orestes, has murdered his mother and finds himself haunted by vengeful spirits called furies who drive him mad with guilt. Terrified, the chorus sing out a desperate prayer: 'I beg you, I beg you,' they sing, 'let Agamemnon's son [that is, Orestes] forget his wild whirling madness.'

What makes this papyrus special is that above the lines are written symbols in Alypian notation. *Orestes* débuted in 408 BC, and there's a good chance that the notes written on this papyrus are from the original performance. That would make this the oldest melody preserved from ancient Greece. Let's take a look at the papyrus.

The notes which are written above the words are from the Lydian mode, but they shift between the enharmonic and diatonic species – a kind of modulation, like shifting in the middle of a song between

C major and C minor. That fits our idea of Euripides as someone who experimented with the new forms of music that emerged in the later fifth century. The change of species might also have given this melody an unsettling or unexpected twist, the way a song's mood can take a sudden turn when it shifts keys in the middle. That would make sense for this song, which is sung during a moment of desperation and unease when things are increasingly uncertain for the characters onstage.

Let's take a look now at part of a modern transcription of this papyrus by the Oxford scholar Armand D'Angour. D'Angour has written the notes which you see on the papyrus into modern sheet music, using staves and noteheads to write the same melody in symbols that any modern musician can understand. The notes with the unusual square heads are the ones we can see written on the papyrus, while the normal rounded ones are the missing notes which Dr. D'Angour has

Fig. 6 Vienna Papyrus (Pap. Vienna G 2315), containing words and musical notation for Euripides' *Orestes* 338–44. Permalink from Austrian National Library: http://digital.onb.ac.at/rep/access/iiif/image/v2/5af078d39f1683785 829f77db4be965359577f6dc708417941693fa76d99941b1a9c87bcbef81bd6fc adb7984bfcbb9b7471f8f9.

filled in using educated guesses based on the trajectory of the melody and some of the more advanced rules of Greek melodic composition (we can't get into those rules here, but you'll find resources for learning more about them at the end of the chapter). Notice the odd notes, though, with little 'up' and 'down' arrows next to them: those are the quarter tones mentioned earlier, the notes that are just a little higher or lower than they could be played on the piano keyboard.

The repeated word *kathiketeuomai*, which means 'I beg you' or 'I pray', is sung on a sequence of notes separated by very small intervals – this creates a creeping, ominous sort of sound which fits with the mood of the song. Altogether, the notes Euripides selected and the way he moves between them – the whole harmonic profile or 'tonality' of the piece – creates an auditory atmosphere which amplifies the meaning of the words and gives them powerful emotional impact which they wouldn't have if they were simply spoken without melody.

What's the point?

That fact helps answer one last important question with which we can close out this chapter: why bother doing this at all? There is so much that is uncertain in reading ancient music. We don't know exactly how these words would have been pronounced, or what dynamic choices the actors might have made onstage. We have lost all the nuance of live performance and the tiny subtleties of feeling, impossible to capture in writing, which would have made the experience of Greek music what it is. Often it is even difficult to tell the exact tuning of a song, especially when we only have a few lines as in this papyrus.

So If we want to recover anything like the sound of these songs, we have to do some guesswork. We have to use our careful reading of theorists like Aristoxenus, as well as more descriptive writing which tells us how people reacted to this music in its day, to imagine how the gaps in our knowledge might have been filled in. But if it's just guesswork, what's the point?

12

Euripides Orestes Chorus

Verses 338–344 from *Orestes*, composed c. 408 BC by Euripides (c. 480–406 BC)

Reconstructed by Armand d'Angour (2016)

Fig. 7 Modern transcription of the Vienna Papyrus by Dr. Armand D'Angour (Oxford University).

To start answering that question, consider this: when we write about the ancient world we are always, no matter what, filling in gaps. Hopefully our guesses get more and more educated as we go along, but there are vast oceans of information that we simply don't have, even outside the realm of music: when we read Greek tragedy, for example, we only read a tiny fraction of the innumerable plays that were performed on the Athenian stage (let alone all the drama that went on outside Athens). Most of those plays are completely gone – not a single copy survives. Given that we live more than 2,000 years after the ancient Greeks, it is a small miracle that we have managed to preserve and unearth as many of their cultural achievements as we have. We have lost much more than we have saved, and we owe what does survive to a massive intergenerational feat of intellectual collaboration: for centuries these texts were copied down, hidden away, corrected, misplaced, and rediscovered. It took a lot of work and a lot of luck.

But it was worth it, because it's worth knowing where we came from. For better or for worse – usually for better – we live today in a world filled with societies that have been inspired by ancient Greek writing and thought. By learning from authors like Plato and Aristotle, by arguing with them, even by misunderstanding them or misinterpreting them, modern cultures all over the world have formed their own ways of life and government in response to the Greeks. Whether we adore the results of that process, or despize them, or a little bit of both and everything in between, we will engage more effectively with the world around us if we know about the complicated story of how it came to be. The society of fifth-century Athens – in all its complexity and variegation, in all its inheritance from the other societies that lived around and before it – remains powerfully present with us. We retain foundational elements of Greek life today, right down to the basic structure of the scales we use in music.

And those scales are an important kind of cultural heritage, because they are a *different* kind than what we get from written words. Take an analogy from another genre: when we read a book, we learn information about what Greek writers, especially rich elites, thought. But when we look at a sculpture, then we actually see something that a Greek sculptor saw – it's a visceral, sensory experience that brings the ancient world a little bit more to life. But not many people know that scientists have recently discovered traces of ink and paint on marble sculptures from antiquity. That is, the art which we usually think of as cold white marble was once painted in bright, living colour. When scholars analyse those traces of ink, they come up with careful, educated guesses about the way ancient art once looked – they are able to re-paint Greek sculptures in something like their original hues. The result may not be exactly accurate, but it is probably quite close to the truth. And it is a vivid, shocking way to experience antiquity – a new way to see the world as the Greeks did, as colourful and alive.

What painted sculptures do for the eyes, musical reconstructions do for the ears. Maybe these tunes aren't exactly right; certainly there is lots about them we will never know. But they take us a small step closer, not just to knowing about ancient Athens, but to *feeling* and experiencing the ancient world in a visceral way. Music, as we'll continue to see, was everywhere for the Greeks. It coloured their experience of every day and seeped into their subconscious minds. It made their experience of the world what it was. We will never be able to share that experience entirely, but making educated guesses at it is, in some sense, what the study of Classics is all about. Listening carefully for echoes of Greek music adds another dimension to our understanding of a culture which remains enduringly important and foundationally influential for the modern world. It is well worth a few guesses and a lot of work.

Some further reading

The known surviving documents of ancient Greek music can be found in a handsome edition from 2001, edited by two experts in the field, Egert Pöhlmann and Martin L. West (*Documents of Ancient Greek Music*, Oxford: Oxford University Press). Check out their introduction (pp. 5–7) for a very short history of the documents and their publication in modernity.

The introduction to Volume 2 of Andrew Barker's *Greek Musical Writings* (Cambridge: Cambridge University Press, 1989, pp. 1–27) contains another helpful explanation of how Greek scales work.

Barker has also written a somewhat more challenging book, *The Science of Harmonics in Classical Greece* (Cambridge: Cambridge University Press, 2007), which explores the intellectual history presented in this chapter in much greater detail. Still more challenging, but also more cutting-edge, is Stefan Hagel's *Ancient Greek Music: A New Technical History* (Cambridge: Cambridge University Press, 2009).

If you'd like to see a video of the song from *Orestes* being performed live, along with a number of other reconstructions from Greek antiquity, you can watch this YouTube video (which, I'm afraid, features the author of this book): https://www.youtube.com/watch?v=4hOK7bU0S1Y.

Rhythms

What is rhythm?

Here is an English sentence:

'I wish I never saw your stupid face.'

Most native English speakers, reading these words, will naturally incline towards a particular pattern of emphasis when doing so:

'I **WISH** I ne-ver **SAW** your **stu**-pid **FACE**.'

The parts in bold are called 'stressed' syllables: they're portions of the word which are meant to be pronounced with more emphasis. Native speakers of English learn which syllables to stress naturally, without thinking about it. But anyone who stops to consider the alternatives will realize how bizarre they feel:

'I wish **I** ne-**VER** saw **YOUR** stu-**PID** face.'

Pronouncing the sentence that way would feel profoundly unnatural, because the 'stress accent' (the special force and volume applied to certain syllables over others) is a crucial part of correct English pronunciation. Even though certain stresses (the stress applied 'stu' in 'stupid,' for example) are often less forceful than others (e.g. the stress applied to 'wish'), the basic structure and pattern remains loosely fixed.

English poets often arrange the stress accents of their words into a regular pattern called 'metre.' This example sentence fits into one of the most common metrical patterns, called 'iambic pentameter.' In this pattern, every line of poetry contains ten syllables which alternate between stressed and unstressed: da-**DUM**, da-**DUM**, da-**DUM**, da-**DUM**, da-**DUM**: 'I **WISH** I **ne**-ver **SAW** your **stu**-pid **FACE**.' Or take a famous line from the great English playwright Shakespeare, who often wrote in iambic pentameter: 'if **MU**-sic **be** the **FOOD** of **LOVE, play ON**.' Even within that pattern there's huge range for variation in composition and performance (the actor pronouncing the line may well also emphasize other words like 'play,' as I've indicated). And English poetry offers a huge array of other patterns as well. But this basic rule remains the same: taking the normal stress accent of everyday English speech, poets arrange their words in a particular sequence so that they conform to a regular order.

Now, though, consider this famous chorus from 'The Battle Hymn of the Republic':

> 'Glory, glory hallelujah!
> Glory, glory hallelujah!
> Glory, glory hallelujah!
> His truth is marching on!'

In each of those repeated lines, certain syllables must be held out longer than others for the song to sound correct: in the first 'glory' of each line, for example, the 'glo-' is longer than that of the second 'glory.' And '-lu-' in 'hallelujah' is longer than 'ha-,' '-le-,' and '-jah' in every line where the word appears.

A syllable's length in time – its 'duration' – is of course a separate thing from its stress. Unlike stress, syllabic duration in English-language songs doesn't develop naturally out of speech patterns: no speaker in normal conversation would say 'Glooo-ry, gloo-ry haaa-le-luuuu-jaaaah!'

So, when we sing songs in English, we stretch syllables out longer in time, or compress them into a shorter space of time, than we would when speaking. But just as in poetry, we tend to keep the normal stress accents from speaking and simply arrange them into a regular pattern. So in addition to the syllable durations, the song we've been singing has regular stresses as well:

> '**GLOOO**-ry **GLO**-ry **haaa**-le-**LUUUU**-jaaaah!'

This combined pattern of stress accent and syllable durations in music is called 'rhythm.'

Ancient Greek poetry also had metre, and Greek music also had rhythm, just as do English music and poetry. But the spoken language of ancient Greek was different from English in some important ways that affect how Greek rhythm works.

There are no set rules in spoken English for how long or how short to hold out each vowel sound – that is, spoken English syllables have a set stress accent, but not a set duration. But in spoken Greek, there are fairly strict set durations for each vowel sound. Some vowels are always long, some are short, and some change length depending on the word. When a vowel is called 'long' in Greek, it really is long – that is, it is meant to be pronounced for a longer time than short vowels.

Even if a vowel is naturally short in and of itself, though, it can be 'lengthened' when it is followed by two consonants in a row. So, in the Greek word *en* (ἐν), which means 'in,' the 'e' sound is short. But if it is followed by the word *de* (δέ), which means 'and,' then you get *en de* – the 'e' sound is now followed by two consonants in a row, 'n' and 'd' (it makes no difference that there's a space between them). Those two consonants lengthen the 'e,' so when spoken the phrase would sound a bit like 'e-en de.' (There is a list of which vowels are naturally long, which are naturally short but may be lengthened by positioning before two consonants, and which may be different depending on the word, in the appendix at the end of this chapter.)

In everyday speech, these differences in vowel duration were probably quite casual. But in poetry, they became strictly formalized: long vowels were meant to be held out for precisely twice as long as short ones. Poets arranged their long and short vowels into patterns, and those patterns were the basis of Greek poetic metre.

This is one of the major differences between English poetry and ancient Greek poetry. English poems take the natural stress accents of spoken language and arrange them into metrical patterns. But Greek poetry takes the natural *vowel durations* of spoken languages and arranges them into metrical patterns.

Here is a short example from one of Homer's poems. The *Odyssey* begins with these famous lines (as translated by Emily Wilson):

'Tell me about a complicated man.
Muse, tell me how he wandered and was lost
when he had wrecked the holy town of Troy . . .'

Those words could be written in Greek something like this:

μοῦσα, ἔννεπε μοι ἄνδρα πολύτροπον, ὃς μάλα πολλὰ πλάγχθη ἐπεὶ
Τροίης ἱερὸν πτολίεθρον ἔπερσεν.

(mousa, ennepe moi andra polutropon, hos mala polla planchthē epei
Troiēs hieron ptoliethron epersen).

These words, with long syllables written in bold and short ones written
in regular type according to the rules of Greek metre (or 'scansion'),
would be pronounced as follows:

Mou-sa **en**-ne-pe **moi an**-dra po-**lu**-tro-pon, **hos** ma-la **pol**-la
planchthē e-**pei Troi-ēs** hi-e-**ron** pto-li-**eth**-ron e-**per**-sen.

This is how the words would be pronounced in everyday speech. But to
give poetic shape to them, Homer arranged them in a particular order
so as to fit their long and short syllables into a pattern. And so the actual
first lines of the *Odyssey*, as originally composed, are as follows:

ἄνδρα μοι ἔννεπε, μοῦσα, πολύτροπον, ὃς μάλα πολλὰ
πλάγχθη, ἐπεὶ Τροίης ἱερὸν πτολίεθρον ἔπερσεν.

When you speak the words aloud now, they sound like this:

And-ra moi **en**-ne-pe **mou**-sa po-**lu**-tro-pon, **hos** ma-la **pol**-la
planch-thē e-**pei Troi-ēs** hi-e-**ron** pto-li-**eth**-ron e-**per**-sen.

Standard notation for Greek scansion uses one symbol (˘) for
short syllables and another (–) for long syllables. Another symbol (x) marks
an 'anceps,' the indeterminate syllable which sometimes falls at the end
of lines (since there are no consonants which follow to determine
syllable length). Written out this way, these first two lines of the *Odyssey*
look like this:

– ˘ ˘ | – ˘ ˘ | – ˘ ˘ | – ˘ ˘ | – ˘ ˘ | – x
– ˘ ˘ | – – | – ˘ ˘ | – ˘ ˘ | – ˘ ˘ | – x

Or, in modern rhythmic notation, they look like this:

Now there's a pattern: each of the lines is broken up into six units (called 'feet') with either one long and two short syllables (a 'dactyl': – ˘ ˘) or two long syllables (a 'spondee': – –). This is one of the most common ancient Greek poetic metres, 'dactylic hexameter.' It is the metre that was used for epic poetry like Homer's – poetry of myths and gods, ancient wisdom and foolish heroes. This was the rhythm in which the Greeks told their oldest stories. It was the heartbeat of their ancient legends.

In her translation, Emily Wilson has changed Homer's Greek dactylic hexameter into a loose English iambic pentameter ('**Muse, TELL** me **how** he **WAN**-dered **and** was **LOST** …). Because English uses stress-accent metres, and because iambic pentameter is the metre we use to write our own epic poetry, this is one quite common way in which translators transfer the feel of Homer's poetry into English. It makes the English sound to us like high legend and ancient myth, somewhat as the Greek must have done to its original audience. What's lost, however, is the musical feel that comes of arranging rhythmic patterns rather than stress patterns.

From words into music

This Greek approach makes for a somewhat different way of thinking about poems than moderns may be used to. At least in English-speaking countries, we often make a distinction between something called 'poetry,' which is written down in the pages of books, and 'music,' which is sung and played on instruments. Of course, we might read poetry aloud and appreciate the metrical sounds of its words. And we often 'set' poems to music – by which we mean taking written words and composing a melody or instrumentation to go along with them. But in general we separate these two things and call them different art forms.

The ancient Greek language doesn't distinguish music from poetry in quite the same way. The Greek art of *poiētikē* (which is where we get our English word 'poetry') literally means simply the art of 'making.' A 'poet' was a craftsman: someone who put things together in an artful way to make an expressive depiction. And the three 'materials' that poets in Greece were supposed to 'make' their compositions out of were language (*logos*), rhythm (*rhythmos*), and melody (*harmonia*). According to Aristotle, whose theory of *poiētikē* is partially preserved in a very influential book called *The Poetics*, anyone who uses one or more than one of those media to depict something qualifies as a poet. So chanting words in rhythm, playing a wordless tune on the pipes, or singing a song along to the lyre all counted in ancient Greece as types of poetry. And poetry itself was considered one form of *mousikē*, music.[1]

What this suggests is that music for the ancient Greeks wasn't just a specialized art form – something you watched one evening at a performance on a concert stage and then didn't think about again until the next show. Instead, Greek *mousikē* was a way of giving artistic form to everyday speech, which already had a kind of musical quality to it. Rhythm was how the Greeks took the vowels of spoken language and arranged them into something aesthetically pleasing, usually by imposing a basic pattern onto them and then playing around with that pattern to give it fluidity and variation.

There were a few basic rules that went into making rhythmic patterns. As already discussed, every vowel had an assigned length. That length could be measured in terms of a unit called the *mora* (plural *morae* – the Greek word usually used here is *chronos*, plural *chronoi*). A short syllable (˘) lasts for one *mora*, while a long syllable (–) lasts for two. Depending on how fast or slow a song was performed, the *mora* could last as long as needed in absolute time – it could be half a second long, or two seconds long, so long as every *mora* in a given stretch of song lasted the same amount of time.

In modern music, a *mora* corresponds to what is called a 'beat': every rhythm is made up of a certain number of beats that can be played fast or slow, as long as they're regular. This too is apparent from the Battle Hymn: in the phrase 'glory, glory hallelujah,' the whole line is divided up into two groups of four equal beats: '**ONE**, two, **three**, four, **ONE**, two, **three**, four' (where bold syllables indicate stress, not length). Tapping those beats out while singing the song reveals that the syllables '-lu-' and '-jah' last two beats each, whereas the syllables 'ha-le' take up just one beat between the two of them. But the beats themselves stay the same throughout, a regular pulse behind the words.

The same goes for our example from the *Odyssey*, which is in dactylic hexameter rhythm. Each foot (where a 'foot' is the smallest repeated unit of arranged syllables) contains four *morae*: two for every long syllable, and one for every short syllable. And just as one can tap out the beat when singing an English song, one can tap out the *morae* when singing or reciting in Greek. So the first line of Homer's *Odyssey* would begin (with long syllables in bold):

And-ra moy | **en**-ne-pe | **mou**-sa po- |-**lu**-tro-
pon, | **hos** ma-la | **pol**-la:

onetwo-three-four | onetwo-three-four | onetwo-three-four | onetwo-
three-four | onetwo-three-four | onetwo-threefour

But stress isn't absent from Greek poetry either. As noted, in English music the beats are arranged according to duration, but they are also given a regular stress which is made to match up with the natural stress accents of speech. Greek music did have something like stress, but it's a little unclear from our surviving sources how exactly it worked. The technical terms here are *arsis* and *thesis*, which literally mean 'lifting up' and 'putting down.' Somehow these two terms refer to a kind of emphasis not unlike stress accent in English. They might have originally referred to dance steps: perhaps the *arsis* was the part of the rhythm where dancers would lift up their feet, and the *thesis* was the part where they would place them down on the ground. Or else the *thesis* would be marked out specially by percussion players – a regular emphasis beaten on the drums or with a pair of castanets.

What we know is that each foot in a Greek rhythm is split into an *arsis* and a *thesis*. Most scholars think that, however it was marked, the *thesis* was the moment of greater emphasis – like a stressed beat or 'down-beat' in modern music (as opposed to the less forceful 'up-beats', which would correspond to the *arsis*).

If I use a colon (:) to mark the split between *arsis* and *thesis* (this split is called the *diaresis* in Greek), we can see that there are three basic ways to divide feet:

1. A foot can have an *arsis* and a *thesis* of equal duration. Dactylic feet are like that: both *arsis* and *thesis* are two morae long (– : – or – : ˘ ˘).

2. A foot can have an *arsis* which is twice as long as its *thesis*, or a *thesis* which is twice as long as its *arsis* (that is, *arsis* and *thesis* can be in a ratio of 1:2 or 2:1). A good example of this is the iambic foot (˘ : –).

3. A foot can have an *arsis* and *thesis* in a ratio of 2:3 or vice versa (3:2). A good example of this is the paeonic foot (– : ˘ ˘ ˘ or ˘ ˘ ˘ : –).

Almost all Greek metres were made by combining feet of these three basic kinds. Sometimes the combinations were simple – like dactylic hexameter, in which every foot is the same pattern. There's an *arsis* and a *thesis*, both two *morae* long. But musicians also made more complex patterns by putting these three basic kinds of foot together into bigger, more elaborate feet – these were called 'compound' or 'mixed' feet. For example, they could put two iambic feet together into one big foot, like this:

˘ – : ˘ –

The result is iambic-style subsections arranged into a dactylic pattern because the *arsis* and *thesis* are equal: they're each three *morae* long. That's why this foot is called an 'iambic dactyl' by Aristides Quintilianus.[2]

There are all sorts of other ways to build up variations on these basic patterns. For example, feet which usually contain a long syllable (–) can be broken up or 'resolved' into two short syllables (˘ ˘), because both arrangements take up the same number of *morae*. Sometimes, a single short syllable (˘) can be lengthened or 'dragged' out into a long syllable (–), often to make the line more expressive or emphasize a particular word.

Take as an example the iambic trimeter rhythm, which contains three iambic dactyls. This is the rhythm that was used for speeches in Greek tragedy:

˘ – : ˘ – | ˘ – : ˘ – | ˘ – : ˘ –

Here's a line from Sophocles' famous play *Oedipus the King* which follows this pattern exactly. King Oedipus has met with a group of terrified subjects on the steps of the Theban altars, and he notes that the whole city is echoing 'with hymns and groaning prayers for help':

˘　–　:　˘　–|　˘　–　:　˘　–|　˘　–　:　˘　–

ὁμοῦ　δὲ παιάνων τε καὶ στεναγμάτων·

homou : de pai-|-anōn : te kai | stenag:matōn

But here's another line from Euripides' *Bacchae*, in which a different king, Pentheus, hears rumours of a foreign visitor to his city of Thebes who is 'wine-faced, with the charms of Aphrodite in his eyes' (line 236):

–　–　:˘　–|　–　　˘　˘:˘　˘　˘|˘　–　:˘　–

οἰνῶπας ὄσσοις χάριτας Ἀφροδίτης ἔχων

oi-nō:pas os-|-sois cha-ri:tas af-ro-|-di-tēs : e-chōn.

This is the same fundamental pattern of iambic trimeter, but with all sorts of ornaments and variations layered into it. The first syllable of the first foot ('oin') and of the third ('-sois') are long, even though those syllables are usually short (this is sometimes called 'drag,' because the actor would drag the syllable out longer than he normally would otherwize). And usually the second half of the third foot is a long syllable, but here it has been 'resolved' into two shorts: 'cha-ri.' Even more daringly, the whole fourth foot consists entirely of short syllables, because Euripides has resolved the second syllable into two without dragging the first: '-as af-ro-'. It's fairly uncommon to find a line with this many variations, but Euripides is especially known for his rule breaking. And indeed all Greek composers played around with rhythm to some degree, switching up the usual structure to give their pieces nuance and variation.

Mixing it up

Using these tools, Greek musicians were able to create an enormous array of complicated rhythms – many more than we can list here. One particularly important one, though, will help give a sense of the wide variation that was possible. The form of rhythm called the 'dochmiac' was often used for songs sung in tragedy by the chorus. In its basic form, the dochmiac foot looks like this:

⌣ – : – ⌣ –

It's a compound rhythm, because it's made up of two smaller units: the iamb (which has three *morae*: ⌣ –) and the cretic (which has five, like the paeonic foot: – ⌣ –). But in practice, this basic pattern can be broken up with drags and resolutions, just as in iambic trimeter. The choral song from Euripides' *Orestes* which we studied in the last chapter was written in dochmiacs. Take these two lines, for example, in which the chorus cry out to the goddesses 'who preside over grim festivals with tears and wailing':

⌣   – : – ⌣   –| ⌣ ⌣ ⌣ : ⌣ ⌣ ⌣ –
ἀβάκχευτον αἲ θίασον ἐλάχετ᾽ ἐν

⌣ ⌣ ⌣ : – – ⌣ –
δάκρυσι καὶ γόοις

a-**ba:cheu**-ton **hai** | thi-a-son : e-la-chet᾽ **en**
da-kru-si : **kai** go-**ois**

The first line starts with a fully regular dochmiac, but then Euripides resolves the long syllables into a string of short ones – this gives the prayer a frantic, staccato sound which conveys the chorus' agitation and distress. Dochmiacs are often used to create that kind of mood, in fact, which is one of the reasons they're a good rhythm for a tragic chorus.

Rhythm contributes a lot to the mood of a song. Consider the stately wedding march (by the nineteenth-century composer Felix Mendehlssohn) that is often played when brides walk down the aisle. It's in a slow, steady rhythm which gives it a feel of majesty and ceremony. Compare that to the driving, agitated beat of a song like Kanye West's 'Heartless': the lurching sway of Kanye's notes makes perfect sense for his lyrics, which are about betrayal and the anguish of heartbreak. But that kind of rhythm would feel completely out of place at a wedding procession: the timing of notes in a song alters the way it can make its listeners feel. Similarly, the clipped staccato of Euripides' resolved dochmiacs makes, by and large, for a more desperate unrest than the regular heartbeat of Homer's dactylic hexameter. (This is to speak very generally of course – variations within a rhythm can often make more difference than variations between different kinds of rhythm. There is room in Homer's dactylic for plenty of frenzied aggravation, just as there is for a wide variety of other moods.)

One important component of the emotional atmosphere created by a rhythm is how fast or slow the song is played. The modern term for this is 'tempo,' and the Greek term is *agōgē*.[3] So far, we've seen that the metrical structure of a Greek song can tell us the relative lengths of each syllable: long syllables last twice as long as short ones. But *agōgē* dictates how long in absolute time to hold out each syllable. If I am performing a dactyl, does the long syllable last for a whole second, or a quarter of a second? That length will determine how quickly the song proceeds, which in turn will help shape the song's rhythmic feel. Consider a song like Joni Mitchell's ballad of love and loss, *Both Sides Now*. When she was a young woman in 1969, Joni recorded this track at a lilting, moderate tempo that gave the song a wistful, reflective tone. But then, in 2000, an older Joni recorded the same song at a slower tempo, giving the song a mournful feeling of loss and regret. The same song, with the same rhythmic structure, sounds extremely different at different speeds.

That's a bit of a problem for reading Greek music, because the Greeks didn't leave behind a way of writing down the *agōgē* of a song. A reader can tell the basic rhythmic pattern of most Greek songs by analysing the metre of the words. And there was rhythmic notation which showed how the rhythm worked if it wasn't obvious from the syllable lengths involved (if the composer had taken liberties, for example, or if the song had an instrumental melody without words). But the speed at which the rhythm ought to be played was something that performers decided for themselves, without ever leaving written instructions that we know of. Much of the time, we have to guess what the *agōgē* would have been from the style and mood of the piece overall.

This is another area where we've lost a lot. In the previous chapter, I mentioned some of the little details of performance that can't be captured in written form: the scoops and grace notes of a pop singer, for example, or the special finesse with which Timotheus must have bent the pitch on his lyre just so. These are the ineffable nuances that make live music what it is, and we are always going to have to imagine them when we think about Greek music – we can never go back and hear exactly how they would have sounded. Rhythm is like that too: in modern recordings like those of the jazz artist Miles Davis, for example, the performer hangs back on the beat in a unique and idiosyncratic way, staying in tempo but using his perfect feel for the song to give his playing a laid-back, self-confident vibe. There's no way to nail that kind of rhythmic intuition down, no way to capture it in symbols: it has to be heard and felt.

We know that Greek musicians took some liberties with their playing, and that there was plenty of space even in the formal rules of Greek metre for experimentation. Some vowel combinations, for example, could be pronounced as a single sound (a phenomenon called *synecphonesis* or *synizesis*) or as a succession of separate sounds (*diaresis*). Achilles, the great hero of Homer's *Iliad*, has the title *Pē-leus* (Πηλεύς: 'son of Peleus'). In its basic form that word has two syllables, both long. In the first line of the *Iliad*, though, Homer uses a different grammatical form, compresses some of the vowel sounds together through *synecphonesis*, and separates others through *diaresis*, to get *Pē-lēi-a-deō*, which in this case is pronounced 'pē-lē-i-a-dyo' (– – ˇ ˇ –) so that it fits into the dactylic rhythm.

It is often easier to grasp how this sort of thing works and makes sense in practice by comparison with modern examples. Shakespeare's history play, *Henry V*, begins with an invocation: 'O, for a Muse of fire, that would ascend / The brightest heaven of invention.' To make the iambic pentameter work, the actor has to pronounce the word 'fire' as one syllable: *fahr*. But in Billy Joel's song 'We Didn't Start the Fire,' the same word ('fire') has to be pronounced with two syllables to fit the rhythm: *fah-yer*. It's the same word, but different artists make changes to the vowel sounds depending on what they need rhythmically. The same is true in Greek music: sometimes, as with Homer, we can see some of the changes made to stay in rhythm. But a lot of those changes were probably too subtle and performer-specific to make their way into the written record.

Writing it down

Some basic rhythmic variations *could* be notated, though. We can see some of that notation at work if we look at another piece of ancient music. Unlike the *Orestes* chorus, this song wasn't written on papyrus: it was carved into a stone column which marked a grave in an ancient town called Tralles (located in modern Turkey). It's not as old as the Euripides: it dates from sometime roughly around 100 AD, when the Roman Empire was in command of the region. Mostly, the rhythm follows the usual pattern laid out by the vowel lengths of the words. Since those lengths would have been obvious to the ancient reader, there's no notation needed unless a vowel is being stretched out to a longer duration than its usual length. In those cases, the writer uses two symbols to show the unusual length:

— means that a syllable should be held for two *morae*, whatever its original length

⌐ means that a syllable should be held for three *morae*, whatever its original length

The only other symbol here is the dot or *stigma* (·), which marks out the *arsis* and distinguishes it from the *thesis*. So, reproduced here are a

Fig. 8 The Seikilos stele, a gravestone carved with words and notation for a short commemorative song. Inharecherche, Wikimedia Commons. https://creativecommons.org/licenses/by/2.0/deed.en.

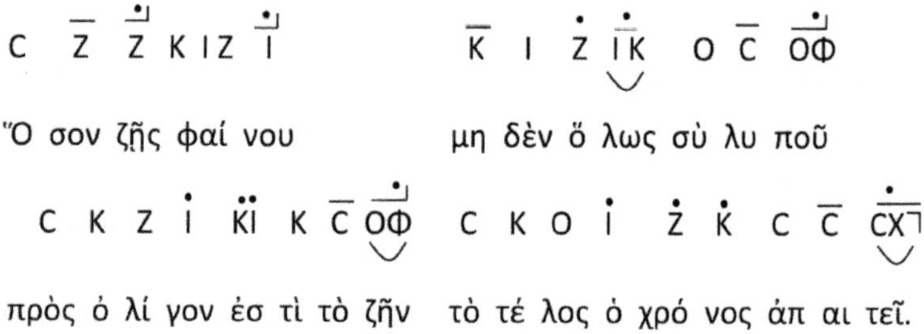

C　Z̄　Z̈ KIZ Ï　　　　　K̄ I Ż ĪK O C̄ O̅Φ̇

Ὄ σον ζῆς φαί νου　　　μη δὲν ὅ λως σὺ λυ ποῦ

C K Z İ K̈ı̇ K C̄ O̅Φ̇　C K O İ Ż K̇ C C̄ C̄X̄⌐

πρὸς ὁ λί γον ἐσ τὶ τὸ ζῆν　τὸ τέ λος ὁ χρό νος ἀπ αι τεῖ.

Fig. 9 Text transcription of the Seikilos stele. Spencer Klavan.

ho - son   zees   pai - noo   mee - den ho lōs -   su lou - poo - ou.

Pros o - li - gon es -   ti   to   zee-een;   to te los ho chro-nos   ap - ai - te - ee - ee.

Fig. 10 Musical transcription of the Seikilos stele. Spencer Klavan.

picture of the column, a transcription of its ancient notation, and a transcription of the same tune in modern notation.

The basic metre of this piece is iambic dimeter: two feet to each line with the *arsis* on the second half of each foot (˘ – : ˘ – | ˘ – : ˘ –). But some vowels have been stretched out to three *morae* (like '*zēs*', '*phai-*', and '*-nou*' in the first line), and some of the places where there would normally be long syllables have been resolved into two shorts (like the '*-oli-*' in *pros oligon*, 'for a little while'). As long as each line has two feet of six *morae* each, with alternating *arseis* and *theseis* of three *morae* each, the pattern stays recognisable. And some of the irregularities help contribute to the mood: for instance, when the poet says that life only lasts 'for a little while,' the string of short syllables on *pros oligon* gives a sense of a swift little life rapidly tripping towards its conclusion. The artistry of the rhythm adds to the song's poignant mood.

We can notice something else important about this epitaph, too. Even at this much later date and in this city far from Athens, people were still using the Greek scales and the Alypian system of notation. There are some differences in style – the tune is quite a bit simpler, for example, and the subtle quarter tones we talked about in the previous chapter seem to be falling out of fashion.[4] But the basic tetrachords and rhythms of Greek music have stayed the same all over the Mediterranean. As we've seen throughout this book, Greek music found its way far from Greece and lasted for centuries after the heyday of Athens.

Appendix: vowel lengths

For those interested in the basic rules for which Greek vowels are long or short, here's a rough-and-ready guide (there are more detailed suggestions in the 'further reading' section).

The long vowels are:

1. Omega (ω, capital Ω), which sounds roughly like the English 'oh' sound in the word 'tone' or 'grow' – written throughout this chapter as 'ō'.
2. Eta (η, capital H), which sounds roughly like the English 'ay' sound in 'hay' or 'prey' – written throughout this chapter as 'ē'.

These vowels and the syllables containing them are always long, no matter where they appear in a sentence.

The short vowels are:

1. Epsilon (ε, capital E), which sounds roughly like the English 'eh' sound in 'step' or 'get'.
2. Omicron (o, capital O), which sounds roughly like the English 'o' sound in 'hot' or 'not'.

These vowels are always short, but the syllables containing them may be long if they are followed by more than one consonant.

The changeable vowels are:

1. Iota (ι, capital I), which sounds roughly like the English 'ih' sound in 'sit' or 'pin'.
   - Iota is short in some words, like *kurios* (κύριος), 'lord,' and long in others, like *sitos* (σῖτος), 'grain.'
2. Alpha (α, capital A), which sounds roughly like the English 'ah' sound in 'car' or 'art'.
   - Alpha is short in some words, like *patēr* (πατήρ), 'father,' and long in others, like *pas* (πᾶς), 'all.'
3. Upsilon (υ, capital Υ), which has a very thin 'oo' sound like the French *tu* or *déjà vu*.
   - Upsilon is short in some words, like *huper* (ὑπέρ), 'above,' and long in others, like *kurios* (κύριος), 'lord.'

Some further reading

Andrew Barker's *Greek Musical Writings* Volume 2 (Cambridge: Cambridge University Press, 1989) contains a translation of Aristides Quintilianus' *On Music* with a helpful introduction and notes (pp. 392–535). The sections which deal with rhythm are Book 1, Chapters 13–19.

The complicated issue of *arsis*, *thesis*, and which one represents which kind of emphasis, has been the object of much recent speculation. For an outline of the issues, an essay by Thomas J. Mathiesen called 'Rhythm and Meter in Ancient Greek Music' from the journal *Music Theory Spectrum* (volume 7, 1985, pp. 159–80) may be helpful. Tosca Lynch has recently challenged the traditional approach, however, by arguing that *arsis* was actually the point of greater emphasis: '*Arsis* and *Thesis* in Ancient Greek Rhythmics and Metrics' (*Classical Quarterly* volume 66, 2016, pp. 491–513).

Stefan Hagel has also recently done some work analyzing the rhythmic notation found in a series of ancient music practice exercizes called 'Bellerman's Anonymi' – see his essay, 'Ancient Greek Rhythm' in *Quaderni Urbinati di Cultura Classica* (volume 88, 2008, pp. 125–38).

For a very clear and accessible introduction to the most important rules of Greek metre, see Martin West's *Introduction to Greek Metre* (Oxford: Clarendon Press, 1987). It's an abridgement of his more comprehensive book, *Greek Metre* (Oxford: Oxford University Press, 1984), which is also excellent for more in-depth analysis.

Dionysius of Halicarnassus also wrote an essay *On Literary Criticism* in which he discusses the relationship between poetic metre and musical rhythm at some length – see especially his Chapter 17.

Beyond Greek Music

Round about 870 AD, a man was born in a place called Farab. Farab is in the northern region of what is now called Iran, but in time the man would travel to Baghdad in Iraq and on to Damascus in Syria. As is often the case with famous scholars of the Near East from this period, this man is known today primarily by his *nisba* – the part of his name that comes from his place of origin. So by and large Abū-Nasr Al-Fārābi is today known to Western scholars, if he is known at all, simply by the name of Al-Farabi. Al-Farabi wrote a great deal, and in particular for us it is important that he wrote a book about music.

Al-Farabi came of age in a place and a time that was richly abundant with Greek philosophy. Already by the fourth and fifth centuries AD, works of Aristotle and others had been translated into Syriac (a language closely related to Arabic and Hebrew, used by many Christians in the ancient Near East). In the Mesopotamian cities of Edessa and Nisibis, Syriac centres of Greek learning sprang up and carried on the tradition of philosophical scholarship that had emerged in the Greek and Roman world after the Classical period. Islam, which emerged and became dominant in the Arab world during the seventh and eighth centuries, flourished in a culture that was already pretty well-versed in the Greeks.

Classical learning in Arabic really took off under the 'Abbasids, a Muslim dynasty which ruled from 750 to 1258 AD. So by the time Al-Farabi was on the scene, Aristotle and his intellectual descendants were well respected and widely disseminated, available in good translations for careful study. In this context and as a deep scholar of both Greek and Muslim strains of thought, Al-Farabi wrote treatizes on logic, language, metaphysics, and mathematics.

By this point it will have become clear that the Greek philosophical tradition places music under the heading of mathematics and considers it one of the ways in which our human ears can gain access to the deeper truths that undergird the universe. This is why, as part of his examination of mathematics, Al-Farabi wrote a book called the *Kitāb al-musiqā al-kabīr*, or *The Great Book of Music*.

The Great Book of Music is a work of music theory by a practising musician. Al-Farabi, much like Lasus of Hermione and the great early theorists of Greek music, was a performer himself. He played the oud, which is a pear-shaped stringed instrument not unlike a lute (and which, legend told, dated back to the grandson of Adam, the first man).

The Great Book of Music devotes careful attention to the *maqāmāt* (singular *maqām*), which are tuning modes somewhat analogous to the Greek ones studied in Chapter 7. Each *maqām* uses a particular series of intervals to dictate which notes are and are not in tune. This is a system that belongs entirely to Arabic music, although like Greek music it places great emphasis on fourths and fifths as the intervals which support the basic structure of each scale. As a musician and a scholar, Al-Farabi was entirely at home in his native tradition.

But he also learned from the Pythagoreans. The *Great Book of Music* is probably most famous among Western scholars for its use of mathematical calculations to define and delimit the intervals that fit well into a good scale. The Pythagorean preoccupation with music as a maths problem, and with harmony as the sound of well-organized proportions, is alive and well in Al-Farabi's writing.

At the same time, we can see him struggling with some of the issues that vexed Aristoxenus, too. Aristoxenus inspired the Greek tradition which insists that what we hear, and not the numbers we crunch, has the last word when it comes to musical beauty. This is particularly apparent when Al-Farabi talks about the semitone: he has difficulty reconciling the intervals which he knows sound beautiful in practice, with the more mathematically strict prescriptions of Pythagorean theory which would advize different intervals than the ones that actually work.

Music is beautiful in its orderliness, but it's also sometimes messy in its beauty: these two contrasting truths of ancient Greek philosophy about music made their way deep into the intellectual bones of this

Arab scholar from the ninth and tenth centuries AD. Like so many of the greatest Greek musical thinkers from whom he learned, Al-Farabi was a thinker and an artist, with a philosopher's insistence on precision but a musician's sensitivity to nuance.

The point of mentioning Al-Farabi's story here is to demonstrate that the musical history in this book is not just a collection of academic tidbits of niche interest for the curious. It is the story of ideas and traditions that radiated outward from ancient Greece to take hold all over the globe, long after Athens was no longer at its height and in places where Greek life and society would have seemed very alien indeed. Greek music transcended those cultural barriers, helping to inform the work and thought of artists and scholars half a world away. But the scholars who took Greek musical thought forward, and the musicians who heard the echoes of Greek music, weren't just slavish imitators producing carbon copies of a bygone tradition. They were freestanding intellectuals and artists in their own right, with deep wells of local tradition and ancient cultures of their own to draw from. The flux and flow of musical practice moved in and out of Athens – from the Levant, from Babylon, from Israel, from what is now Italy – often congregating in that one cultural hub, but always coming from further afield and destined to travel outward again into distant parts of the world.

World music: Greek thinking goes abroad

Various chapters of this book have noted examples of Greek musical notation, philosophy, and practice popping up in the unlikeliest of places. Besides Al-Farabi, there was an epitaph with Hellenistic Greek poetry and accompanying musical symbols in what is now Turkey, probably from the first or second century AD. There were Romans from the twilight of the republic and the Empire who picked up the Pythagorean philosophy of musical cosmology – and thinkers from Kepler to Shakespeare who picked up those same ideas in the modern period. And of course there was more: our earliest Christian hymn – from around the third century AD – is also written in Greek, with Greek notation, on a scrap of papyrus discovered in Oxyrhynchus, Egypt. The success of Greek systems for writing and thinking about music was so great that few regions of the world remained untouched by some part of Greek musical thought in the end.

Then there are parts of the ancient Greek musical heritage – most notably the living tradition of playing Greek scales on Greek instruments – which have pretty much died out. Some scholars will argue that Greek tunings did survive, although in radically modified form, because the early Christian church preserved a few vocal melodies and transmitted them all the way down to the seventh, eighth, and ninth century when the form of Christian singing known as Gregorian chant began to take shape. That tradition, in turn, was the foundation upon which modern Western music was laid, so if it does have real ancient Greek influence then there would be a direct line from, say, Euripides to Bach and on through to the Backstreet Boys.

That kind of idea is a stretch, though. Because between the papyrus scribblings of the early Christian Church and the first examples of written Gregorian chant, there's a yawning chasm of several centuries during which no written music, that we know of, survives in the West. Most scholars agree that the actual, living tradition of Greek music died out long before modernity really began in earnest.

What didn't die were the ideas, many of which survive and even have some currency today. Pythagorean philosophy, in particular, got a grip on the world's imagination. It's part of why we still analyse our scales in terms of numerical ratios, breaking them down into fourths and tetrachords as we did with the Greek scales in Chapter 2. Pythagorean mathematical ideas, as filtered through Plato, made their way into Roman philosophy and on outward throughout the world, reaching all the way to the Arab Muslim world of Al-Farabi.

There was no more powerful exporter of Greek musical ideas – indeed, of Greek ideas of any kind – than Rome. From a philosophical standpoint, we've already seen how this was true with Cicero and Boethius. They weren't alone – even Lucretius, a contemporary of

Cicero's and a follower of the Greek philosopher Epicurus (who didn't have a very high opinion of music) sounded almost like Damon or Aeschylus when he wrote in his poem *On the Nature of Things* that when the Gauls go into battle, 'the hollow pipe inflames their minds with Phrygian measures.'[1] No matter your philosophical allegiances, if you were an intellectual in Rome there was a good chance you had absorbed a few bits of conventional wisdom about the emotional and psychological power of music.

But that wasn't all – the Romans picked up musical practices from the Greeks, too. Roman *tibiae*, as we saw in Chapter 2, are basically identical in their basic form to Greek *auloi*, and like the *auloi* they were used routinely at parties and in the theatre. Horace, a hugely popular poet and another one of the erudite commentators who frequented the same circles as Cicero and Lucretius, wrote a long poem called the *Art of Poetry* in which he grumbled about how elaborate and showy pipe music in the theatre had become.[2] The developments he was lamenting were Roman, but in attitude and preferences he sounded a lot like Plato – keep it simple, he insisted, and don't let the crowds tell you how you should sound. The Greeks passed down everything from their music, to their ideas of and elite tastes in music, to the Romans.

Horace had something to say about that too, something we've already quoted: 'conquered Greece conquered her savage captor.' As Greece fell politically under Roman sway, Rome and her upper classes became infatuated with Greek culture to the point of obsession and self-deprecation. Cicero himself was a prime example: 'in education and, in fact, in every kind of literature, Greece outdid us. It was easy to do when there was no competition,' he wrote in his *Tusculan Disputations*.[3]

But even in these cases, Greek music was never carbon-copied for mass reproduction. The Romans had a musical culture of their own, one that would take a book of its own to explore. Horace's little tirade in the *Art of Poetry* bears witness to the fact that there were cultural developments going on in Rome that took Greek musical instruments and ran with them. Rome was also a key player in the ongoing story of how music came from all over the world into Athens and flowed outward from there to take on innumerable new forms around the world.

This has been a book about an important moment in music history. An underappreciated moment, one whose antiquity has obscured many of its most important details and so made it hard to really see for what it was. But a pivotal moment, all the same, in the chain of events that is human artistic history. Like the poetry of England in the Romantic era, or the films of America in the early twentieth century, the music of Athens in the Classical period represented a profusion of creativity, the convergence of older ideas and practices from around the world to produce something profound and radically new.

Such moments never stand alone. The Romantic poets studied folk song and German philosophy; the freshness of their vision nourished the imagination of J. R. R. Tolkien and inspired countless musicians to set their words to music. The American directors of cinema's 'golden age' cut their teeth watching continental film and emulating the masterpieces of the European stage; their influence is visible in the work of later greats like Martin Scorsese, Quentin Tarantino, and the Coen brothers. So, too, Greek musicians – who in many cases came into Athens from cities far afield in Sicily, the Argolid, or Anatolia – created a hotbed of culture and thought whose consequences would be felt for generations.

Classical and contemporary musicians, scientists, philosophers – people from every walk of life and all over the globe have found in Greek musical heritage a wellspring of inspiration and instruction. Every time we open iTunes, or go to a concert, or even look through a telescope, we are rubbing shoulders with the Greeks and their intricate, complicated legacy. The Athenians and their diverse disciples left only the faintest traces of their actual music behind. But they gave us a uniquely sophisticated set of tools for contemplating and appreciating that vast interconnected web of melody, motion, politics, mystery, and emotion that they called *mousikē*. Music – that strange and powerfully communicative kind of sound which compels us all, and the countless forms of life it engenders and accompanies – has always been with us. And Greek music, after all these years, is with us still.

Some further reading

Al-Farabi's *Great Book of Music* has not been fully translated into English, although Alison Laywine of McGill University is working on an edition. Meanwhile, there are partial translations by Geert Jan van Gelder and Marlé Hammond (published in 2008 by the Gibb Memorial Trust as part of *Takhyîl: The Imaginary in Classical Arabic Poetics*) and one in a doctoral dissertation by Azza Abd al-Hamid Madian (1992, *Language–Music Relationships in Al-Farabi's 'Grand Book of Music'*). There is also a French translation by Rodolphe d'Erlanger, reprinted in 2001 by Geuthner.

A number of other modern scholars are quite interested in Al-Farabi, among them Charles Butterworth (who wrote a useful essay in 2013 called 'How to Read Alfarabi,' which was collected in *More Modoque*, a book published by the Forschungszentrum für Humanwissenschaften der Ungarischen Akademie der Wissenschaften).

To understand Roman music in its own right, you can't do better than Timothy J. Moore of Washington University in St. Louis. His *Music in Roman Comedy* was published in 2012 by Cambridge University Press.

Notes

Chapter 1

1 These are far from the only sources available to us, as will become clear. The compendious *On Music* of Aristides Quintilianus, from somewhere between the first and third centuries AD, and the treatize of the same title falsely ascribed to Plutarch, probably from the late second century AD, will appear frequently in these pages, as will a range of other works.

2 This is a quotation from Pericles' famous 'Funeral Oration,' a speech he gave to commemorate those who had died in the first year of the Peloponnesian War (in the winter of 431–430 BC). The words are recorded – not verbatim, but with probable accuracy in the major outlines and ideas – by the historian Thucydides in his *History of the Peloponnesian War* Book II, Chapter 38.

3 This inscription can be found described and translated in Daniel David Luckenbill's *Ancient Records of Assyria and Babylonia* (Chicago, IL: University of Chicago Press, 1926), Volume 2, p. 38.

4 This quotation is taken from a composition of Pindar's of which only a little bit has survived on a scrap of mutilated papyrus – in the scholarly catalogue of Pindar's works, it is known as Fragment 125.

5 Sappho is often referred to this way in what is called the *Palatine Anthology* (sometimes abbreviated as *AP*), a collection of ancient Greek verse compiled over the years and assembled in one manuscript by Constantine Cephalas in the tenth century AD (later altered slightly to become the *Greek Anthology*). See, for example, Book 7, Poem 14; Book 9, Poem 66; and Book 9, Poem 571.

6 Sappho's work comes down to us in fragments; this one survives because it is quoted in a commentary by the fifth-century-AD philosopher Syrianus. It is traditionally numbered as Fragment 105(a) as in the standard English edition of Edgar Lobel and Denys Page.

7 This information comes from Hellanicus, who kept a record of oral tradition and local history on Lesbos in the fifth century BC. He is quoted by Athenaeus, a man of letters who lived during the second and third centuries AD.

8   This is what we learn in a biography of the Archaic Spartan lawmaker
    Lycurgus, written by Plutarch, a first-century-AD essayist (Chapter 28,
    Sections 4–5).

9   See Thucydides, *History* Book 5, Chapter 70; Aulus Gelllius, *Attic Nights*
    Book 1, Chapter 11, Sections 1–4.

10 An official script, sometimes called the 'Peisistratean (or Peisistratid)
    recension,' would have been an easy way to keep everyone singing the same
    words – there are various accounts of such a thing in, for example, ancient
    biographies ('Lives') of Homer, and in the second-century-AD *Description
    of Greece* by Pausanias (Book 7, Chapter 26, Section 13).

11 See the records about Lasus in *On the Marriage of Philology and Mercury*
    by Martianus Capella (who reached his peak activity in the early 400s AD),
    Book 9, Section 936, and in the massive tenth-century Byzantine
    encyclopaedia called the *Suda* under the entry for 'Lasus.'

Chapter 2

1   One version of this myth can be found in the *Homeric Hymn to Hermes*,
    which is a narrative poem in the style and metre of Homer (but composed
    later than Homer).

2   This story is recorded by Plutarch in his *Customs of the Spartans*, p. 238c.

3   This story can be found in Plutarch too (*Agis* 10.6; *Customs of the Spartans*
    238c), as well as in a work *On the Fundamentals of Music* by the
    philosopher Boethius (1.1), and *The Learned Banqueters* by Athenaeus
    (p. 628b).

4   See Athenaeus, *The Learned Banqueters* 14.616e–617e and Aristotle's
    Politics 1341a–2b.

5   See *Republic* 399d.

6   See *Politics* 1341a–b and compare Plato's *Symposium* 215b–c.

7   See, for example, Plato's *Laws* 700a–b and Aristotle's *Politics* 1341a.

8   This anecdote is recorded in Athenaeus 616e–617b.

9   This story is retold in Book 1, lines 688–711 of the epic poem
    Metamorphoses by Ovid. Ovid lived from 43 BC to 17 AD. His complicated
    and sexually explicit poetry has made him an object both of fascination
    and censure in the ancient and modern world.

10 Scholars have learned details about the workings of the *hydraulis* from various comments and images preserved in the work of a first-century-BC architect Vitruvius, *On Architecture* (Book 10, Chapter 8), in the *Pneumatica* of the first-century-AD Alexandrian Hero (Book 1, Chapter 42), and in the *Natural History* of the first-century-AD Roman Pliny the Elder (Book 7, Chapter 125), among others.

11 This is from Book 2 of Horace's *Epistles*, Poem 1, line 156.

Chapter 3

1 This moment happens at *Symposium* 176e; for more on the topic, see also Section 9 of another *Symposium* by a contemporary of Socrates and Plato, Xenophon. Compare also Aristotle's *Politics* 1339b, in which the philosopher quotes the Archaic poet Mousaios to back up his claim that 'at their gatherings and pastimes, people bring along music because it can warm their hearts.'

2 See especially Sections 1–3, 7, and 9 of Xenophon's *Symposium*, and compare lines 1177–78 of Euripides' play, *Ion*.

3 See *On Music* Book 2, Chapter 3 – a similar observation is made by the first-century-BC philosopher, Philodemus of Gadara, in his fragmentary work *On Music* (Book 4, column 132 in Daniel Delattre's edition).

4 There are all sorts of references to this kind of trumpeting in the ancient world: for starters, see Thucydides' *History of the Peloponnesian War* Book 5, Chapter 70, Xenophon's *Anabasis* 4.3.29–32, and Aristides Quintilianus's *On Music* Book 2, Chapter 6.

5 This is from Aristophanes' *Frogs*, lines 354–57.

6 These can be found in Aristophanes' *Birds*, lines 159–61, and *Peace*, lines 868–70. See also the *First Oration* by the later rhetorician Himerius (315–386 AD).

7 So says Aristotle in *Poetics* 1449a.

8 Parodies of tragedy are to be found, for example, in *Thesmophoriazousae* 39–69, 95–174. Similarly, the competition between Aeschylus and Euripides in *Frogs* must have contained elaborate mimicry of each playwright's style.

9 This is another one of our musical documents: it is a papyrus catalogued as Pap. Leiden Inv. P. 510.

Chapter 4

1 See Plato's *Republic* 376e and *Timaeus* 88c.
2 See *Deipnosophists* 631b–c. Military training, too, overlapped with dance in the form of the *pyrrhichē*.
3 For expressions of this kind of disdain about overly musical men, see not only Aristotle's *Politics* 1341a–b but also Homer's *Iliad* 3.54 and Plato's *Republic* Book 3, 410d.
4 Plutarch, *Alcibiades* 2.4–5.
5 On the process of selecting boys for these performances, see pseudo-Aristotle's *Constitution of the Athenians* Chapter 56.
6 See especially *Laws* 700e–701b.
7 See, for example, Homer's *Iliad* 18.490–96.
8 Most of this comes from Chapter 14 of Plutarch's *Lycurgus*.
9 This statement is in Aristotle's *Politics* 1339b.
10 See Plato's *Republic* Book 10, 595a and *Laws* Book 2, 670–74.
11 This comes from Pollux's *Onomasticon*, Book 9, Section 41. See also the *Institutes of Oratory* by Marcus Fabius Quintilianus (Quintilian) who taught rhetoric in first-century-AD Rome (Book 1, Chapter 10, Sections 17–18).

Chapter 5

1 Plato, *Republic* Book 4, 424c.
2 These Aristoxenean views are preserved particularly well in pseudo-Plutarch's *On Music* (see especially 1144a–b).
3 Aristotle, *Nicomachean Ethics* Book 2, 1103a.
4 Diogenes' work is partially preserved by an Epicurean scholar, Philodemus of Gadara, in a very damaged papyrus known as the *De Musica* – see 'further reading.'
5 For a few versions of this story, see 'further reading.'
6 Hibeh Papyrus I.13, lines 13–17 – an English translation is available in Andrew Barker's *Greek Musical Writings* volume 1 (Cambridge: Cambridge University Press, 1984), pp. 183–85.
7 See Aristotle, *Poetics* Chapter 4, 1448b; Aeschylus, *Libation Bearers* line 564; Aristophanes, *Frogs* lines 108–15.

8   Plato, *Republic* Book 3, 393d.

9   Dionysius of Halicarnassus, *On Literary Composition* Chapter 11, lines 73–119.

10 See Plato, *Laws* Book 1, 644–45 and Aristotle, *Nicomachean Ethics* Book 3, 1116a.

11 Homer, *Iliad* 3.54.

12 Aeschylus, *Persians* 388–95.

13 Plutarch, *Life of Pericles* Chapter 4.

14 Aristides Quintilianus, *De Musica* 62.20–24.

15 Homer, *Iliad* Book 16, lines 740–42.

Chapter 6

1   This quotation is taken from a large edition which collects the remaining fragments of those 'Pre-Socratic' philosophers. Because the edition was compiled by Hermann Alexander Diels and revised by Walther Kranz, the fragments are numbered according to what are called 'Diels-Kranz (DK) numbers.' This particular fragment is DK 44 B4 (from Stobaeus' *Anthology* 1.21 7a).

2   Andrew Barker (*Greek Musical Writings* Volume 2, Cambridge: Cambridge University Press, 1989, p. 29) notes aptly that the existence of the *harmonikoi* 'dispel[s] the impression that musical theory in [the fifth century] was a Pythagorean monopoly.' His excerpts from the fragments of Archytas (as quoted in Porphyry's *Commentary on Ptolemy's Harmonics*, esp. Sections 56–57) are particularly revealing in this regard: they demonstrate minute attention to the structure, functioning, and material exigencies of instruments and those who use them. Archytas' work is proof that ancient theory and practice did not need to be antithetical to one another, no matter how often they in fact were.

3   See also *Phaedo* 86b and Aristotle's *De Anima* 407b27, 1340b18.

4   This is Book 6 of Cicero's *Republic* (the 'Dream of Scipio'), Sections 18–19.

5   The actual mathematics of tuning had changed somewhat by Kepler's day, meaning that he used not the Pythagorean tunings but a new set of geometric ratios that conformed more precisely to the physical realities at stake.

6   See *Phaedrus* 246a.

Chapter 7

1   In reality, Greek theorists tended to describe their scales from top to bottom. For simplicity's sake, however, this chapter follows the modern convention of starting with low notes and moving up to higher notes.

2   This information is recorded on pp. 1137–40 of a treatize by a later author (called 'pseudo-Plutarch') from the second or third century AD. But many scholars believe that pseudo-Plutarch cites authentic ideas from earlier authors, including Aristoxenus himself (who may have helped record some of the early Greek music history about figures like Terpander).

3   There are two famous inscriptions from a Cretan town called Priansos, recorded in the compendium called *Inscriptiones Creticae* (1.24.7–9), which shows that by the third century Timotheus was numbered among the artists whose music counted as old standards and cherished classics.

4   We should definitely take these stories with a grain of salt. They come from a biography of Euripides by a philosopher and historian called Satyrus, who lived around the third century BC and whose work survives on a papyrus from a trash heap in the Egyptian city of Oxyrhynchus (papyrus number 1176). Later on the biographer and essayist Plutarch would tell similar stories in his *Moralia*, p. 795d. It's more likely that these were tall tales invented to record the closeness between Euripides' and Timotheus' work, than that they were factually accurate recountings of actual collaboration.

Chapter 8

1   Discussions of these ideas and their implications are to be found in Plato's *Republic*, Book 3, 398d (and another dialogue, the *Gorgias* at 501d–2b), as well as Aristotle's *Poetics* Chapter 1, 1447a and pseudo-Plutarch *On Music* 1144a–b.

2   Much of our most useful information on rhythm is found in Aristides' *On Music* Book 1, Chapters 13–19, which attempt to systematize comprehensively the many kinds of rhythm that were theoretically possible in the Greek system. This particular claim, about the iambic dactyl, can be found in Chapter 17. See further the 'Some Further Reading' section at the end of this chapter.

3 This term is used, for example, in the remaining fragments of Aristoxenus' lost work on rhythm, the *Elements of Rhythm* (Section 11) and in Aristides Quintilianus' *On Music* Book 1, Chapter 19.

4 Aristoxenus, apparently, was already complaining in his day that the subtler nuances of small intervals were becoming difficult or impossible for the layman to hear because they were being less commonly used: see pseudo-Plutarch, *On Music* 1145a4–b6.

Chapter 9

1 This is from Book 2, line 620 of Lucretius' poem.

2 This passage can be found at lines 202–20 of the *Ars*.

3 See Book 1, Chapter 1, Section 3 of the *Tusculan Disputations*.

Glossary

Aeschylus see **Tragedy**.

Al-Farabi ninth-century AD philosopher whose *Great Book of Music* shows engagement in the Arabic world with ancient Greek music theory and philosophy.

Aristotle A major fourth-century BC Greek philosopher and disciple of **Plato** who wrote in his *Politics* and *Poetics* about the role of music in society.

Aristoxenus A disaffected student of **Aristotle** and an ex-**Pythagorean**, Aristoxenus made the most complete systematic effort to date in the fourth century BC to define the Greek theory of harmony and rhythm. These efforts are preserved, although not completely, in his *Elementa Harmonica* and *Elementa Rhythmica*.

Athenaeus Greek writer of the late 100s and early 200s AD whose *Deipnosophistae* (*Learned Banqueters* or *Sophists at Dinner*) contains lengthy meditations on music which preserve views from earlier scholars including **Aristoxenus**.

Aulos The most common type of ancient pipe. Usually found in the plural, *auloi*, these pipes were played in pairs and accompanied (among other things) the music of drama.

Barbitos A long stringed instrument, deeper in tone than the *kithara* or *lura*, sometimes associated with revelry and Dionysiac frenzy. Often pictured in the hands of satyrs or other raucous characters, but also associated with some Archaic lyric poets.

Boethius Philosopher of the late Roman empire whose *On the Fundamentals of Music* gives an example of how Greek musical theory and philosophy found its way into later writings and was preserved into modernity.

Cicero Roman statesman, orator, and amateur philosopher of the late Roman republic whose interest in **Plato** and **Pythagoreanism** led him to record various reflections on harmony and so provide an example of Roman interest in Greek music.

City Dionysia see **Dionysia**.

Damon of Athens A 5th-century BC **sophist**, or public intellectual, whose teaching and research were focused on rhythmic forms and (perhaps) the emotional associations they evoked.

Dionysia A major festival, held every year, at which music contests were staged in Athens and tragedies were performed in trilogy.

Dionysius of Halicarnassus 1st-century BC literary scholar, historian, and essayist whose notes on style include key pointers on the pronunciation, accentuation, and rhythmic patterning of the Greek language.

Euripides See **Tragedy**.

Hydraulis An elaborate and probably quite rare manually operated water-organ – the details of its construction are recorded by **Vitruvius**.

Kithara An ornate stringed instrument largely used by professional performers and competitors.

Krotala An ancient form of 'clapper' or 'castanet' held in the hand and used for percussion.

Lasus of Hermione A celebrated sixth-century BC musician and early music theorist who came to Athens at the invitation and under the patronage of Hipparchus, son of **Peisistratus**. He is known for having written down the first-ever Greek book on music, which does not survive.

Lura See **Lyre**.

Lydia An ancient kingdom in the west of Asia Minor (now Turkey) which existed from around 1200 to 546 BC and with which early (Archaic) Greek musicians likely shared many techniques and practices.

Lyre Though this word is sometimes used as a generic term for Greek stringed instruments, it actually translates the Greek *lura*, which in its most technical usage applies only to the most basic form of stringed instrument.

Mousikē The Greek art or arts presided over by the Muses (*Mousai*). Though it included the arts now called 'music' and 'dance' in English, *mousikē* was a broader term also designating such things as mathematics and philosophy.

Music of the Spheres The array of philosophical ideas, many of them Platonic or Pythagorean, which combined in antiquity and afterwards to create a vision of music as interwoven into the entire cosmos and the human soul.

New Music (the) Modern term for an ancient phenomenon in the second half of the 5th century BC. Musicians such as **Timotheus of Miletus** and **Phrynis of Mytilene** (as well as tragedians such as Euripides) experimented with modulation and melodic innovation which elite commentators such as **Plato** found distasteful.

Orestes A **tragedy** by Euripides (performed in 408 BC) from which some strains of choral music are preserved on papyrus.

Panathenaic Games A regular festival which, after **Peisistratus** revitalized it around 566 BC, took place every four years and included major musical competitions.

Phrynis of Mytilene A famous kitharode (ca. 450-420 BC) who performed in Athens and was well-known as a practitioner of the "New Music" which experimented with modulations, melodic runs, and other deviations from compositional tradition.

Plato A major Greek philosopher (ca. 429-347 BC) whose work on music (much of it adopted from **Pythagoreans**) in dialogues such as the *Republic*, *Laches*, and *Timaeus* records some important ancient attitudes toward music's emotional power and place in society.

Plutarch 1st-century AD essayist and biographer who preserves a number of anecdotes about major figures in Greek and Roman history.

Peisistratus A 6th-century BC Athenian ruler who seized total control of the city-state, reorganized the **Panathenaic Games** (in 566 BC) and City Dionysia (in 534/531) and made other efforts to unify Athens and consolidate its reputation as a major Mediterranean power.

Psaltērion A triangular harp with strings of unequal length. Possibly originating in **Lydia**, these were one of the more frequently used stringed instruments after the **Lyre**, ***Kithara***, and ***Barbitos***.

Pythagoras A mystic, scholar, and philosopher from the 6th century BC who wrote nothing down, but whose followers contributed much to the mathematics of harmony and the philosophy of cosmic music.

Sophists A group of public intellectuals who were hugely influential and important during the 5th century BC in Athens. Their work mostly does not survive, but it was the backdrop against which much of the philosophy which does survive was formulated.

Sophocles See **Tragedy**.

Terpander A semi-legendary *kithara*-player credited with (among other things) winning the first-ever *kithara* competitions at Sparta's Carneia festival.

Timotheus of Miletus A fifth-century BC composer who was known in Athens for his transgressive experiments with melody and instrumentation. He may have collaborated with Euripides.

Tragedy A form of musical theatre for which Athens was known and in which it hosted competitions every year at the **Dionysia**. The three major writers of tragedy whose work survives in the present day are (in chronological order) Aeschylus, Sophocles, and Euripides.

Index